THE HILL

THE HILL

An Illustrated Biography of Syracuse University

1870–Present

JOHN ROBERT GREENE

With a Foreword by Chancellor Kenneth A. Shaw

Majestic swells the graceful Hill
From Onondaga's vale.

—from a song composed by George W. Elliot, Class of 1873

Syracuse University Press

The paper used in this publication meets the minimum
requirements of American National Standard for
Information Sciences—Permanence of Paper for Printed
Library Materials, ANSI Z39.48-1984.

LIBRARY OF CONGRESS CATALOGING-IN-PUBLICATION DATA

Greene, John Robert, 1955–
    The Hill : an illustrated biography of Syracuse
University, 1870–present / John Robert Greene.— 1st ed.
        p.   cm.
    Includes index.
    ISBN 0–8156–0648–6 (alk. paper)
    1. Syracuse University—History—Pictorial works.
I. Title.
LD5233.G74 2000
378.747'66—dc21   00–024998

JOHN ROBERT GREENE is Paul J. Schupf Professor of
History and Humanities at Cazenovia College, where he
has taught since 1979, and lectures at Syracuse University's
University College. His previous books include *Syracuse
University: The Eggers Years* (1998), *Syracuse University:
The Tolley Years, 1942–1969* (1996), and several books on
twentieth-century presidencies, most recently *The
Presidency of George Bush* (2000).

Designed by Christopher Kuntze
PRINTED IN CANADA

For

PATTY, T. J., CHRISTOPHER,

and MARY ROSE

Publication of this book is made possible by a generous gift from Elaine '42 and Joseph Spector '38, LAW '41.

Contents

Hendricks Chapel.

Foreword

KENNETH A. SHAW

A university is many things, of course—a place to study, to learn, to teach, to create new knowledge, to dream, to fall in love, to be frustrated, to fail, to succeed, to mature, and to begin again.

Syracuse University is such a place. In a series of historical volumes by W. Freeman Galpin and then by John Robert Greene, words capture a portion of this place. Numerous videotape productions tell us more. And now here is an illustrated history to continue the story.

Even in a time when electronics gives us whirling images and incredible special effects, still photographs have an important place. They can be savored and retrieved for times of quiet reflection.

These pictures tell the story of Syracuse University, a dynamic institution, which through good times and bad has held firm to its core values of quality, caring, diversity, innovation, and service. But more important, in each of these images are a host of memories for generations of Syracuse graduates, faculty, staff, and friends.

I invite you to relax and take a leisurely trip through our past and our present. This is your university.

Author's Note

The vast majority of the text that accompanies
this volume is based upon the five volumes of
Syracuse University (Syracuse: Syracuse
University Press, 1952–98; specific volumes are
referred to in the text), as well as the clippings
file of the Syracuse University Archives. Use is
also made of the author's interviews with many
luminaries of the period from 1942 to 1992, done
for the last two volumes of the above history.

Unless otherwise credited in this volume, all
photographs are taken from the collections of the
Syracuse University Archives, the Syracuse
University Photo and Imaging Center, the
Syracuse University Office of Special Events, the
Syracuse University Office of News and
Publications, the files of the *Syracuse Record*, or
the Syracuse University Department of Athletic
Communications, and are the property of
Syracuse University.

The author would like to thank Joe Glisson for
permission to include several of his cartoons
from *Dome, Sweet Dome: A Syracuse and
National Sports Cartoon Retrospective* (1996).

A View from the Heights

I have two favorite views of the Syracuse University campus. One is the highest point of my commute into the university area from my home in the nearby village of Chittenango. From the corner of Ostrom and Waverly Avenues, driving between DellPlain and Booth Halls, one is treated to a wonderful vista, where the university's grandest buildings—Crouse College, the Hall of Languages, and the Carrier Dome—dominate the scenery. The second, more select view is from my office window on the sixth floor of Bird Library. That view is filled with the grandeur of Lyman Hall. It seems that, like myself, everyone's favorite view of the campus looks high across its panorama, as it sits high upon a hill just to the south of the city of Syracuse (note, for example, the favorite view of Chancellor Kenneth A. Shaw, told to me during the interview that is reprinted in chapter eight). Indeed, most alumni and supporters of the university simply refer to our alma mater by the title of this book: "The Hill."

Campus view: from corner of Ostrom and Waverly Avenues.

I share this with you because my original desire to write this volume came from my belief that the Syracuse campus is one of the most eclectically beautiful in the nation, and there was no photographic essay available to alumni and friends of the university that allowed them to keep and enjoy that beauty. But this work evolved into something above and beyond the presentation of the university's best pictures of itself. We are indeed fortunate to be one of only a few colleges in the nation to have produced a multivolume history of itself. However, there had yet to be written a *one-volume* history of the university—one that could offer us a reasonably concise view of our past. Using the organization provided by the first five volumes of the university's history, two of which I wrote, and using those volumes as the basis for the text included herein, I believe that this book now provides that one-volume look at our history to the present day.

Campus view: from author's office, sixth floor, E. S. Bird Library.

Thus, what I hope I have accomplished in this volume is to offer an illustrated history of Syracuse University. I addressed both the choosing of the photographs in this volume and the writing of the accompanying text with the goal of showing, through pictures, the life story of an institution that has continued to be vibrant since the day of its founding 130 years ago.

I most certainly did not do it without help. In at least five separate departments, and in the private collections of many of its schools and colleges, the university has archived or otherwise preserved over two million photographs, putting it on a par with any of the presidential libraries in the National Archives system. The bulk of the photos, however, was chosen from three separate archives. The first is the Syracuse University Archives, located in the E. S. Bird Library. The archives have been my part-time home for the past five years of research and writing, and I am genuinely grateful for the assistance—and the remarkable willingness to ignore many of my last-minute-before-deadline requests—of my friends Edward Galvin and Mary O'Brien. Second is the photo archive in the university's Photo and Imaging Center. Were I to give individual credit for each photograph in this volume that was taken by Steve Sartori, the university's photographer, I would have had to list his name more than two hundred times. Let me do so here, and pay tribute to his skill as an artist—in many ways, the later chapters of this book are as much his as they are mine. His assistant, Dale Luckette, was also of inestimable help. The third repository is the vast number of photos taken for the Publications Office; navigating me through that material was my friend Carol North Schmuckler. I also want to thank Kevin Morrow and Anna Toole of the *Syracuse Record*, Mary Jane Nathan of the Office of Special Events, and the staff of the Syracuse University Department of Athletic Communications, especially Marlene Ouderkirk.

I was particularly fortunate to have, once again, the services of an outstanding research assistant. Martha Papworth, a student at Cazenovia College, provided sage background research, a keen eye for a good photo, and an indefatigable sense of balance and humor throughout this project.

It is not in the nature of any writer—or any other artist, for that matter—to trust anyone with his or her work. However, I was quick to learn that in any photographic essay, one must trust the gifts of those artists who conceptualize and lay out the design of the book. I am fortunate to have a wonderful relationship with my friends at Syracuse University Press, and I knew from my earlier books that the work of production manager Mary Peterson Moore and designer Kit Kuntze was some of the best in the business. I think that the reader will be appreciative of their talents—it is truly a handsome book. Press director Robert Mandel and marketing manager Theresa Litz have believed in my writing from the start, and I am thankful that they continue to do so.

By his support of this latest volume, Chancellor Kenneth Shaw has once again showed his unwavering commitment to the preservation and the publication of the history of this university. While the chancellor gave me his support, his assistant, Marlene Carlson, got me everything else I needed; over the past four years, not one word of my work would ever have seen the light of day had it not been for Marlene's support. Lansing G. Baker, Senior Vice President for University Relations, has supported this project since its inception. I also continue to be grateful beyond words for the support of Cazenovia College, my home institution, in all of my writing and publishing efforts. Particular thanks are due to former president Adelaide "Van" Titus, dean of the college, Michael Fishbein, and Dr. Timothy McLaughlin, chair for the Center of Natural and Social Sciences.

But, once again, no one gives me the support that I get from my family. I dedicate this book to them, as I have dedicated all of my books over a fifteen-year writing career.

Chittenango, New York   JOHN ROBERT GREENE
January 2000

THE HILL

The Establishment of "Piety Hill"   1870–1893

Hall of Languages, ca. 1880.

Leadership

Rev. Daniel Steele, 1871–1872

The former president of Genesee College, Steele was named professor of mental and moral philosophy, and vice president of the new college. He served as the first administrative head of the university before the selection of its first chancellor.

Alexander Winchell, 1872–June 1874

Trained at Wesleyan University, Winchell had served as the president of Masonic University in Selma, Alabama, and had taught geology, zoology, and botany at the University of Michigan from 1855 to 1872. He oversaw the funding and the building of the Hall of Languages. Following his year as chancellor of Syracuse University, he taught at Vanderbilt and at Michigan, where he died in February 1891.

Rev. Erastus O. Haven, June 1874–1880

A distinguished educator, Haven had served as president of both Northwestern University and the University of Michigan. He had also served as a member of the Massachusetts State Senate and as an editor of a Boston newspaper. In 1880, elevated to a bishopric, Haven left the Hill.

John R. French, Summer 1880–April 1881

Born in Pulaski, New York, French had studied at Hamilton and Wesleyan Colleges, and had been a secondary teacher, a lawyer, and a professor of mathematics at Genesee College—a position he would hold for twenty-six years at Syracuse University. A popular teacher who also served as dean of the College of Liberal Arts, French was the natural choice to serve what would be the first of two stints as interim chancellor. He again served as chancellor pro tempore in fall 1893.

Rev. Charles N. Sims, April 1881–1893

Born in Fairfield, Indiana, and educated at Indiana Asbury University and Ohio Wesleyan, Sims served as principal of several Methodist seminaries, as pastor of several churches, including Summerfield Methodist Church of Brooklyn, and as president of Valpariso Male and Female College before coming to Syracuse in April 1881. Following his tenure as chancellor, Sims served as the pastor of churches in Indianapolis and Syracuse, where he died in 1908.

Rev. Daniel Steele.

Alexander Winchell.

Rev. Erastus O. Haven.

John R. French.

Rev. Charles N. Sims.

Founding

On May 1, 1832, the Genesee Wesleyan Seminary opened its doors in Lima, New York, with a program designed to prepare students for college. With its success, in 1852 the Methodist Conference opened a college in Lima that emphasized agriculture. In August of that year, a college hall was dedicated. It was, from the start, beset with financial difficulties.

Genesee Wesleyan Seminary, erected in 1842.

Genesee College Hall, erected in 1852.

It was the assessment of many in the conference that if a college were to survive in New York State, the Lima site would have to be abandoned. Despite the protests of the residents of Lima, a group of Syracusans made a pitch for the college to be moved to their city. Their key selling

Reference: W. Freeman Galpin, *Syracuse University.* Volume I: *The Pioneer Days.* Syracuse: Syracuse University Press, 1952.

points: a location close to the railroad and the promise of a strong financial base. When the state of New York refused to approve the relocation of the college from Lima, the determined group of Syracusans petitioned for a college of their own. At a meeting in February 1870, Bishop Jesse Truesdell Peck promised a $25,000 endowment to the yet-unchartered school. This donation set off a spate of giving; it was these donations that turned the tide. On March 24, 1870, the state of New York granted Syracuse University its charter. Peck was elected the first president of the Board of Trustees.

Bishop Jesse Truesdell Peck.

The first classes were held on September 5, 1871, in the upper floors of the Myers Block, on the southeast corner of Montgomery and East Genesee Streets, opposite the present City Hall. The Myers Block location would serve the university until the 1873 opening of the Hall of Languages.

The Myers Block.

Student body and members of the staff at Syracuse University, 1871.

The first property actually *owned* by the institution was the old St. Charles Hotel—also called the Remington Block and then the University Block—on West Washington Street (between Bank Alley and South Warren Street).

The old University Block. The photograph was taken from an advertisement for the university; the lettering shown was never actually on the building.

The new University Block.

It would become the most recognizable building in the history of the university. The cornerstone for the Hall of Languages, the first building built at the university, was laid on September 1, 1871. It was built on a fifty-acre tract of land overlooking the city of Syracuse that had been donated to the university by George F. Comstock. Constructed out of Onondaga limestone at a cost of $136,000 (a $200 profit from the hayfields surrounding the building helped pay for part of the original mortgage on the building), "HL" was dedicated on May 8, 1873. For its class gift, the Class of 1885 provided the funds for the installation of the clock on the north side of the building.

"The dowager queen of the campus."

Michael O. Sawyer, on the Hall of Languages

Hall of Languages, ca. 1880.

Hall of Languages, early 1900s.

Hall of Languages.

Growth

Under its first two chancellors, Syracuse barely held on. Its third chancellor, Charles Sims, brought the institution back from debt: he inherited a deficit of $173,000, and by 1893, the university was operating at a $6,775.84 surplus. He also oversaw the creation of the institution's first endowment. In 1881, the combined registration in the three colleges of the university (Liberal Arts, Medicine, and Fine Arts) was 322 undergraduates; by 1893, that number had jumped to 763, largely as a result of the phenomenal growth of the College of Liberal Arts.

"[They need a man] to create a university, not to manage one, and they can't afford a Chancellor and Creator both."

Alexander Winchell

Close behind Liberal Arts was the flowering of the nation's first degree-conferring College of Fine Arts. Key to its growth was George Fisk Comfort, who had taught painting and drawing at the Wyoming and Cazenovia Seminaries and at Allegheny College. Comfort built a school that originally centered on the teaching of architecture

Liberal Arts faculty, in the *Onondagan,* 1892.

and painting. Despite the efforts of Chancellor Winchell to close the school, so as to save money in the aftermath of the Panic of 1873, the school prevailed, adding a Department of Music by the 1880s.

Students in biology class, 1888.

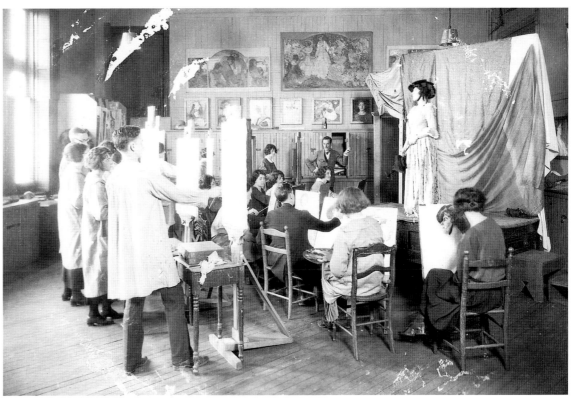

George Fisk Comfort with Fine Arts faculty, ca. 1890.

Art students with model, ca. 1880.

With the growth of the fine arts on the Hill came the need for its own building. Help came from trustee John Crouse, a Syracuse merchant and banker, who not only donated the monies for the building that bears his name but also personally supervised every phase of the project, living for a period of time with his architects. Built at a cost of $500,000, the John Crouse College of Fine Arts, dedicated on September 18, 1889, housed a Roosevelt organ run by a ten-horsepower Baldwin engine (which powered the six bellows for the organ's seventy-four stops and 2,591 pipes). It also housed the beautiful Crouse Chimes.

John Crouse College of Fine Arts.

Crouse College, auditorium and organ.

First school of medicine.

Graduates of the school of medicine, 1876.

Delta Kappa Epsilon, Classes of 1888, 1889, 1890, and 1891, at chapter house, 1005 East Genesee Street (1888). Pictured: George H. Maxwell (back row, seventh from left, in mustache)—member of Class of 1888 and future patron of the Maxwell School of Citizenship and Public Affairs.

The third of the university's initial colleges was a transplanted one. When the Geneva (N.Y.) College Medical Facility came upon hard times in 1871, an agreement was reached to move it to Syracuse University. The College of Physicians and Surgeons of Syracuse University opened its doors on October 3, 1872; its first location was in the Clinton Block. In 1875, it moved into its new home on the Hoyt Property on Orange (McBride) Street. One of the buildings on the lot, a former carriage factory, was rebuilt to include lecture rooms, a dispensary, and laboratories; the other structure, a former blacksmith's shop, was converted into a chemical lab.

The advent of the hard sciences at Syracuse University was forecast by a donation from Erastus Holden of Syracuse, who underwrote the building of an observatory, which was dedicated

to his son. The Charles Demarest Holden Observatory, opened in the summer of 1887, housed an eight-inch Alvin Clark telescope, a three-inch reversible transit, a comet seeker, a chronograph, and a chronometer.

The first fraternity at the university was carried over from "Old Genesee." The "Syracuse Chapter of the Mystical Seven" appeared in September 1871; in November of that year, it had evolved into Delta Kappa Epsilon. By September of the following year, Alpha Phi had become the university's first sorority. For quite some time, its home, at 17 University Avenue, was the only sorority house in the nation.

Holden Observatory.

Photo of Haley's Comet, taken from Holden Observatory's comet seeker (1910).

The Alpha Phi house, 17 University Avenue, and its parlor, 1890 (from *The History of Alpha Phi International Fraternity, 1872–1930*, New York: The Century Company, 1931).

Athletics

Athletics did not have high priority in the minds of the institution's first chancellors. Sports were played on the "Old Oval," an athletic field located on the site of the present-day quad. The university's original gymnasium was a twenty-by-sixty-foot storehouse located behind HL. Students and alums demanded a new gym, but the university claimed financial stringencies. In an effort to get the administration's attention, in April 1886 thirteen members of the Class of 1889 burned it down. Sims finally asked for a new gym in January 1890; it was completed in December 1891. Located on the site of the present Hendricks Chapel, the gym was divided into two sections: one for men and one for women. It also held a bowling alley and a swimming pool. In 1929, it would be moved to a site between Steele Hall and Archbold Stadium. It was occupied by the School of Journalism in 1953; in 1965, it was demolished.

In June 1872, the first issue of the student newspaper, the *University Herald*, pleaded: "Shall We Boat?" Thanks to the generosity of Charles Holden and George F. Hine, the university's first shell was purchased, and on June 25, 1873, the Syracuse University Boating Association raced in its first regatta. Later that year, the team was reorganized as the "Syracuse University Navy."

On April 20, 1872, the Syracuse University Baseball Association was founded. During this period, poor attendance plagued the Orange nine, largely because they were without a worthwhile field. They played their games on the University Grounds, an area of flat land between Marshall Street and Waverly Avenue. In the early years, the

Gymnasium and athletic field.

SHALL WE BOAT?

Considering the natural advantages, and the material at our command, we would unhesitatingly say, Yes. Some may decry the practice, but they might with equal justness tirade against any other healthful amusement. If there be any objections to boating, they lodge against its abuse, and not its legitimate use. If they oppose Regattas, they might as well rule all emulation out of the world; and if they did, what would be the effect on human effort? It may appear to others as premature, this advocacy of boating, so early in the history of the University. It will certainly do no harm to thus early agitate the matter, for agitation preceeds all action.

University Herald, June 22, 1872.

Hill fielded some rather poor squads—in one game in 1873, for example, the Syracuse nine committed fourteen errors.

"Flies were missed in the most approved manner, whenever the visitors had two men on bases. With all the poor plays, the Hamilton backers were trembling until the game closed for fear Syracuse would make a spurt in spite of their hard luck."

The Syracusan, December 5, 1879

In 1884, the university played its first recorded football game against the Medical College of Syracuse—in essence an intramural affair. No score has survived. Varsity football was established in 1889; the first intercollegiate game was on November 23, 1889 (the Orange lost to University of Rochester, 36-0). In 1890, the 8-3 Orange posted their first victory (against Rochester, 4-0), and their first complete season, under their first coach, Robert Winston.

Baseball team, 1888.

THE BIG ORANGE 1890

Football team, 1890.

First Issues of University Publications

The University Herald, June 22, 1872.

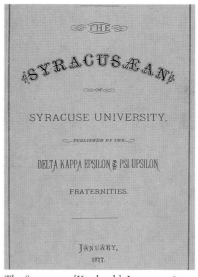

The Syracusan [Yearbook], January, 1877.

The Syracusan, October 14, 1878.

Best Athletic Records of Syracuse University to 1892

Best Athletic Records of Syracuse University up to 1892.

EVENT.	RECORD.	NAME.	TIME.
100-Yards Dash	10 1-5 s	G. W. Hoyt, '93.	June 17, 1890
220-Yards Dash	23 1-5 s	G. W. Hoyt, '93.	June 30, 1891
440-Yards Dash	52 3-5 s	G. W. Hoyt, '93.	June 30, 1891
Half-Mile Run	2 m. 7 s	E. K. Macomber, '93.	June 9, 1891
One-Mile Run	4 m. 55 s	C. W. Tooke, '91	May 24, 1889
One Milk Walk	7 m. 23 s	O. R. Whitford, '90.	May 25, 1887
120-Yards Hurdle	18 s.	F. L. Purdy, '92.	June 30, 1891
220-Yards Hurdle	28 s.	F. L. Purdy, '92.	May 30, 1891
Two Mile Bicycle Race	6 m. 39¼ s.	J. P. Becker, '88	May 25, 1888
Hop, Step and Jump.	43 ft. 4½ in	F. L. Purdy, '92.	June 9, 1891
Standing High Jump	4 ft. 7 in.	F. L. Purdy, '92.	June 17, 1890
Running High Jump	5 ft. 4 in	F. L. Purdy, '92.	April 25, 1889
Standing Broad Jump	9 ft. 9 in.	W. E. Blair, '88	May 12, 1887
Running Broad Jump	19 ft. 11½ in	F. L. Purdy, '92.	May 30, 1891
Pole Vault	9 ft. 2 in	F. L. Purdy, '92.	June 17, 1890
Putting Shot (16-lb)	37 ft. 7¾ in	F. L. Mead, '91	May 30, 1891
Throwing Hammer (16-lb)	90 ft.	F. L. Mead, '91	May 16, 1891
Throwing Base Ball	338 ft	F. C. Seager, '88	May 21, 1880

Best Athletic Records N. Y. State Inter-Collegiate Athletic Association.

EVENT.	RECORD.	NAME AND COLLEGE.	PLACE.	TIME.
100-Yards Dash	10 1-5 s.	Lee, Hamilton	Geneva	May 30, 1891
220-Yards Dash	23 s.	Spurlarke, Hamilton	Albany	May 24, 1889
440-Yards Dash	52 2-5 s.	Strasenburgh, Hobart	Geneva	May 30, 1891
Half-Mile Run	2 m. 5 2-5 s.	Coventry, Hamilton	Syracuse	May 30, 1890
One Mile Run	4 m. 48 2-5 s.	Coventry, Hamilton	Syracuse	May 30, 1890
One Milk Walk	7 m. 32 s.	Whitford, Syracuse	Albany	May 24, 1889
Two Mile Bicycle Race	6 m. 39½ s.	Becker, Syracuse	Rochester	May 25, 1888
120-Yards Hurdle	18 s.	Purdy, Syracuse	Geneva	May 30, 1891
220-Yards Hurdle	27 1-5 s.	Lee, Hamilton	Geneva	May 30, 1891
*Standing High Jump	4 ft. 6 in.	Coville, Cornell	Utica	May 28, 1886
Running High Jump	5 ft. 3 in	Jewell, Hobart / Elwood, Rochester / Hoff, Hobart	Rochester / Geneva / Geneva	May 25, 1888 / May 30, 1891 / May 30, 1891
*Standing Broad Jump	9 ft. 9¼ in.	Morrison, Cornell	Utica	May 28, 1886
Running Broad Jump	19 ft. 11½ in.	Purdy, Syracuse	Geneva	May 30, 1891
Pole Vault	9 ft. 7 in.	Landon, Union	Albany	May 24, 1889
*Throwing Base Ball	323 ft. in.	Hawkins, Syracuse	Utica	May 28, 1886
Putting Shot (16-lb)	37 ft. 7¾ in.	Mead, Syracuse	Geneva	May 30, 1891
Throwing Hammer	86 ft. 3 in.	Mead, Syracuse	Geneva	May 30, 1891

The Onondagan, 1893.

Syracuse University Forum, September 2, 1885.

The University News, December 13, 1887.

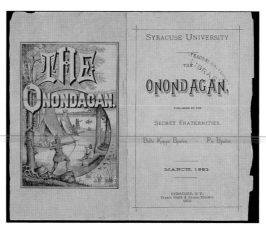

The Onondagan [Yearbook], March 1883.

"I See a Great University on the Hill"   1893–1922

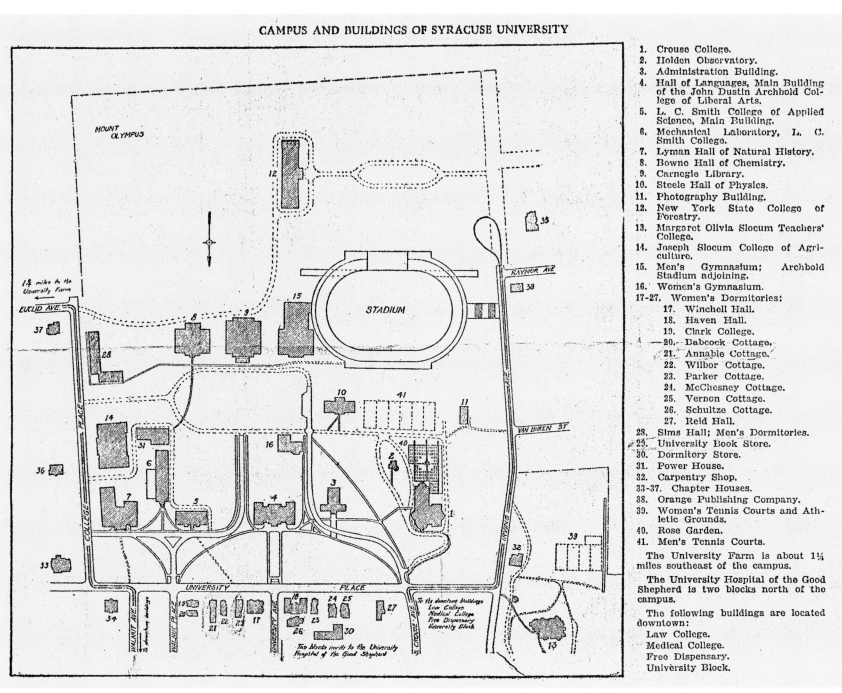

CAMPUS AND BUILDINGS OF SYRACUSE UNIVERSITY

1. Crouse College.
2. Holden Observatory.
3. Administration Building.
4. Hall of Languages, Main Building of the John Dustin Archbold College of Liberal Arts.
5. L. C. Smith College of Applied Science, Main Building.
6. Mechanical Laboratory, L. C. Smith College.
7. Lyman Hall of Natural History.
8. Bowne Hall of Chemistry.
9. Carnegie Library.
10. Steele Hall of Physics.
11. Photography Building.
12. New York State College of Forestry.
13. Margaret Olivia Slocum Teachers' College.
14. Joseph Slocum College of Agriculture.
15. Men's Gymnasium; Archbold Stadium adjoining.
16. Women's Gymnasium.
17–27. Women's Dormitories:
   17. Winchell Hall.
   18. Haven Hall.
   19. Clark College.
   20. Babcock Cottage.
   21. Annable Cottage.
   22. Wilbor Cottage.
   23. Parker Cottage.
   24. McChesney Cottage.
   25. Vernon Cottage.
   26. Schultze Cottage.
   27. Reid Hall.
28. Sims Hall; Men's Dormitories.
29. University Book Store.
30. Dormitory Store.
31. Power House.
32. Carpentry Shop.
33–37. Chapter Houses.
38. Orange Publishing Company.
39. Women's Tennis Courts and Athletic Grounds.
40. Rose Garden.
41. Men's Tennis Courts.

The University Farm is about 1¼ miles southeast of the campus.

The University Hospital of the Good Shepherd is two blocks north of the campus.

The following buildings are located downtown:
Law College.
Medical College.
Free Dispensary.
University Block.

Map of the university, 1922–23.

Leadership

JAMES ROSCOE DAY, November 1893–1922
Born in Whitneyville, Maine, and educated at Bowdoin College, Day was serving the Calvary Church in New York City at the time he was named chancellor. At over six feet in height and more than two hundred pounds, Day was an imposing figure in size and spirit. Inheriting a financial deficit, Day oversaw the first of two great periods of campus renewal in the institution's history. With almost militant abandon, Day transformed Syracuse University from a small liberal arts college into a university capable of competing with other prestigious institutions.

James R. Day.

"When I came to Syracuse in 1919 after two years in the Army, it was my impulse as Chancellor Day came into my first faculty meeting to shout, 'Attention, Commanding Officer,' as we were accustomed to do [on the Western Front]."

Finla Crawford, November 14, 1958

Chancellor Day and students.

Chancellor Day leads commencement procession.

The Building Blitz

When James Day arrived on campus, Syracuse University had a faculty of 60 and five buildings; when he left, the university had a faculty of 350 and twenty-four buildings. Day's building binge would not be surpassed until the 1950s. The phenomenal growth of Syracuse University during the first two decades of the twentieth century can be easily summed up: Chancellor Day's vision, Mr. Archbold's money. Born in Leesburg, Ohio, John D. Archbold was the president of Standard Oil Company of New Jersey. A friend of Day's from New York City, Archbold had sponsored Day for the chancellorship at Syracuse. Of the many things for which Archbold was responsible: the erasure of the loan for the new University Block; funds to help save the crew team in 1910; and the financing of Carnegie Library, a new athletic field (the "New Oval"), a new gymnasium, and a new stadium. In June 1914, the name of the institution's oldest school was changed to the John Dustin Archbold College of Liberal Arts.

John D. Archbold.

Reference: W. Freeman Galpin, *Syracuse University.* Volume II: *The Growing Years.* Syracuse: Syracuse University Press, 1960.

Chancellor Day, in white hat; to his left, John D. Archbold.

"When his task was finished, Syracuse University was essentially the same kind of institution as Northwestern or Southern California or any other nominally denominational university."

William Pratt Graham on James R. Day

"They call me a boss, but you know Teddy [Roosevelt] and I are not afraid of that."

Day to Archbold

Changes in the curricula—most notably the dropping of the all-college requirement in the classics and an increase in the number of electives—contributed to a rapid increase in enrollment. When Day took over in 1893, enrollment stood at 751 students; by the time he left office, enrollment was at 5,600. This enrollment explosion necessitated the building of on-campus residence halls. Female students could live in Winchell Hall—completed in June 1900 at a cost of $30,000—for $3.75 to $5.75 per week—the more expensive rooms had their own private baths. It wasn't long before a second women's hall was needed, because of the many complaints received by the administration about the noise from the daily

Haven (*left*) and Winchell Halls.

practice of music students. Haven Hall was added in 1904; located across University Avenue from Winchell, it housed seventy-eight women.

At the turn of the century, the medical school was more than carrying its own weight in terms of enrollment. It too needed a new, larger home. What would be called the second medical college was built to the north of the old Medical Building on Orange Street at a total cost of $55,000. Dean John Heffron pushed forward with a bold set of programs, which included the construction of a building to house the Syracuse Dispensary, then located on Warren Street. The dispensary, built adjacent to the new medical school on East Genesee Street, was opened and dedicated in March 1914. Heffron also pushed for the purchase of the Hospital of the Good Shepherd, which had been founded in 1872 by Bishop Frederic Dan Huntington of the Episcopal Diocese of Central New York. The purchase was made on May 1, 1915. Later that year, the hospital's School of Nursing became a formal part of the university.

Second medical college and annex.

Syracuse Free Dispensary.

The law school (John Crouse residence).

Machinery Hall and Smith Hall.

Hospital of the Good Shepherd.

A committee had looked at the possibility of creating a law school as early as 1873, but the plan was deferred until after the establishment of the College of Liberal Arts. In 1895, the trustees voted to open a college of law. That fall, the first twenty-three students met in rooms in the Bastable Building (corner of South Warren Street and East Genesee). In the summer of 1898, the law school moved to the western section of the University Block. It stayed in those offices until April 1904, when it moved into the John Crouse mansion on the corner of East State and East Fayette Streets.

Day's greatest contribution to the growth of the curriculum at the university was his expansion of the institution's resources in engineering and in the sciences. In 1896, Lyman C. Smith, founder of the Smith-Corona Typewriter Company and a member of the Board of Trustees, promised to fund a college of applied science at the university—largely to supply trained toolmakers and mechanics for his business. In 1902, thanks to his donation, Smith Hall was built at a cost of $75,000. On the day of its dedication, the L. C. Smith College of Applied Science was also announced. Five years later, Machinery Hall opened as a complement to Smith Hall. Other benefactors supported Smith's interests. Mrs. Esther Baker Steele of Elmira donated $5,000 for the building of a laboratory; Archbold anonymously donated an extra $28,000. Built to resemble Holden Observatory, Steele Hall, which opened in the fall of 1898, was built at a cost of $46,000. Bowne Hall opened in 1909, taking the Chemistry Department out of its cramped quarters in Steele Hall. Lyman Hall, financed by a $200,000 gift from the late John Lyman, a former trustee, was started at the same time as Machinery Hall but not completed until the winter of 1910—it housed the natural sciences.

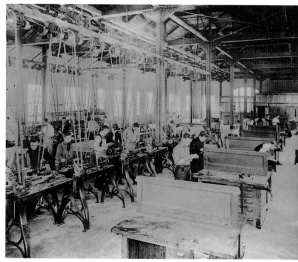

Interior of Machinery Hall.

Lyman Cornelius Smith.

Steele Hall.

Bowne Hall under construction, 1907.

Lyman Hall.

John Lyman.

The first university library was located in the Myers Block building. It was not until the university had procured the library of one of the world's foremost scholars that it undertook the building of a library on the main campus. In 1887, Prof. Charles Wesley Bennett negotiated the purchase of the library of German historian Leopold von Ranke. Bennett had promised the von Ranke family that a suitable building would be constructed to house the collection. It was completed in 1899, at a cost of $34,850.88 (John D. Archbold gave $12,500), and had room for 135,000 volumes. In 1903, a west wing was added.

It was soon obvious that the von Ranke Library was not large enough to house the university's collection, which was growing exponentially as the institution grew. From 1901 to 1905, Day courted philanthropist Andrew Carnegie, who had financed the building of a public library in downtown Syracuse. In 1905, Carnegie donated $150,000 for a new university library with the stipulation that Day match the gift; once again, Archbold gave the largest share of the final amount. Progress was slow, owing to the simultaneous construction of Sims and Lyman Halls and the new gymnasium. Finally, on September 11, 1907, Carnegie Library opened. The former library was turned into an administration building.

Von Ranke Library.

Interior of von Ranke Library, ca. 1907.

Breaking ground for the Carnegie Library, 1905.

Construction of Carnegie Library, 1906.

Margaret Olivia (Mrs. Russell) Sage.

Carnegie Library.

Main Reading Room, Carnegie Library.

The leftover funds from the Carnegie challenge allowed for the building of Sims Hall, which opened in the fall of 1907 on College Place as a men's dormitory. It would, in time, be used for myriad purposes, including housing the engineering program.

In June 1906, the university announced the formation of Teachers College. With the permission of Mrs. Russell Sage, the primary benefactor of the school, the name was changed to honor her mother: the Margaret Olivia Slocum Teachers College. It was housed in Yates Castle, which had been purchased in March 1905 for $50,000. Sitting on fourteen acres on Irving Avenue, the Gothic mansion—complete with its own bridge and "moat"—was referred to after its purchase as Renwick Hall, taking its new name from its architect.

In 1898, the New York State Legislature created a four-year professional school of forestry at Cornell University. However, the project was never adequately funded, and Day quickly stepped into the void. With the help of Louis Marshall, a New York lawyer and philanthropist, the New York State College of Forestry at Syracuse University was approved in July 1911.

Sims Hall.

Yates Castle/Renwick Hall.

Forestry Building / Bray Hall.

Although the school began with only two faculty members—including its first acting dean, William L. Bray—it grew quickly to the point where it needed a building of its own. Construction of the Forestry Building (renamed Bray Hall in 1933) began in April 1914 and was completed for the opening of classes in fall 1917.

"I see in my mind's eye a great university on the Hill. I see a dozen colleges. Instead of several buildings, I see a score of buildings. Instead of a student body of 800, I see a student body of 8,000, and the University as the center of the educational system of the State of New York."

James R. Day, 1895

World War I

Day took the university through two wars—the Spanish-American conflict (1898) and World War I (1917–19). During World War I, Syracuse University, like other institutions of higher education, gave a rousing send-off to its sons who had been drafted for overseas service. On campus, some 1,000 men (including future chancellor William Tolley) received training as members of the Student Army Training Corps. They were trained in telegraphy, automechanics, and other fields. Eighty-one alums and students died in the war, including thirteen SATC members who died in the flu epidemic of 1918–19. In December 1919, following the armistice, Syracuse became the first school to institute a Reserve Officers' Training Corps (ROTC) on its campus.

Drafted men at Archbold Stadium, August 1917.

Army Training Corps students in classroom.

Student Army Training Corps at Syracuse.

Athletics

Unlike his predecessors, Day saw value in intercollegiate athletic competition. Virtually single-handedly, his friend John Archbold took it upon himself to upgrade the institution's athletic facilities. In 1895, Archbold paid for a "New Oval." Dedicated in June 1895, it included an athletic field with a quarter-mile track, batting cages, and a grandstand that held one thousand people—all built at a cost of $7,000.

Archbold also underwrote the construction of a football stadium, built in a natural depression behind Steele Hall. Archbold announced his gift in March 1905; the stadium that would bear his name was completed three years later at a cost of $400,000. Covering a total area of six and one-half acres, the state-of-the-art facility originally seated 20,000. The as yet unfinished stadium hosted its first football game on September 25, 1907 (SU defeated Hobart, 20-0).

Excavation for new stadium, October 1906.

Archbold Stadium, ca. 1908, with construction for Archbold Gymnasium in foreground.

New Oval, 1904.

Day had pleaded with the board to build a new gymnasium, but there was simply too much being built at the same time. In April 1907, spurred on by Archbold's gift of the football stadium, the board finally agreed. The cornerstone of the gymnasium was laid in March 1908, and the gymnasium, butting up against the end of Archbold Stadium, opened sometime in 1909. The total cost was $360,000; Archbold paid off the mortgage that had been taken out on the University Block to finance it.

November 21, 1908: SU 29, University of Michigan 4.

James A. Ten Eyck.

Archbold Gymnasium, 1908.

Team photo of 1922 Orangemen. The team included future SU football coach Reeves "Ribs" Baysinger and boxing and lacrosse coach Roy Simmons, Sr.

"The greatest master-oarsman-creator on the continent."

Day on James Ten Eyck

Football history at SU was drastically altered in 1900, when Cornell University broke its athletic relationship with SU. In its stead, the games with Colgate University took on monumental importance. After the 1915 victory over the Red Raiders, students tore up the campus's wooden sidewalks and built a bonfire (the chancellor made them pay for the damage). Football teams were of uneven quality during the first two decades of the twentieth century; the 1915 team, with a record of 9-1-2, was the best.

Crew had been discontinued from 1885 to 1889, but trustee agitation prompted Day to bring it back. In fall 1902, James A. Ten Eyck was named head coach; thus began seasons of success for the "Syracuse Navy," including a 1908 win at the Hudson Regatta at Poughkeepsie.

Baseball went through some more meager years following the construction of the New Oval. That would change in 1910, with the hiring of Lewis (Lew) Carr. Carr had played alongside Honus Wagner for a championship Pittsburgh Pirates team. In his thirty-two years on the Hill, Carr coached teams of mostly moderate talent. His 1917 team was one of his best, ranked fourth nationally by Spaulding's official guide.

Lewis (Lew) Carr.

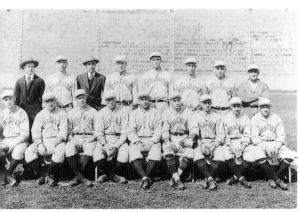

Baseball team, 1918. Coach Lew Carr is seated, front row, fifth from left.

"The iron man of Syracuse University baseball . . . Piety Hill's Lou Gehrig."

Daily Orange, 1939, on Lew Carr

Varsity basketball debuted in 1899. The team played two games that year, against the Christian Association of Hamilton (Ontario) and the Christian Association of Syracuse—they lost both matches, 16-6 and 26-5. Over the next decade, however, the Orange were a respectable 66-53. Then in 1910, the institution retained its first

full-time coach—Eddie Dollard ('08). From 1911 through 1922, Dollard's teams went 132-34, and in 1913–14 the team had a perfect 12-0 season.

Basketball team, 1913.

A lacrosse team was organized in 1917 by Prof. Laurie D. Cox of the College of Forestry. The first intercollegiate lacrosse game was played in 1916 against Penn State; in 1920 the squad captured the first of its many intercollegiate championships.

Intercollegiate championship lacrosse team, 1920.

On January 2, 1898, the first women's basketball game was played on the Hill between the coeds of the Classes of 1900 and 1901. Later that year, a women's team played the university's first intercollegiate game; they visited Cortland and defeated the Normal School, 6-2. The construction of Archbold Gym allowed the old gym to be converted to the Women's Gym. In 1919, nationally known anatomist Katharine Sibley was named the first director of the Women's Gym. In 1928, the Women's Gym was moved from its old site, near the present Hendricks Chapel, to a site near Steele Hall.

Katharine Sibley (*foreground*), with members of the Women's Athletic Governing Board, 1912–13.

Women's basketball team, 1922.

Student Life

When Day came to campus, there were six fraternities and four sororities; by 1907, there were twenty-five fraternities, along with sororities and various new honor societies. The rather conservative chancellor attempted to curb what he called the "passions of youth" by changing rush rules and by attempting to enforce curfews and limits on the number of dances and mixers that were held. He was only moderately successful.

Phi Gamma Delta party, ca. 1905.

The Dekes: Delta Kappa Epsilon, ca. 1915. Photograph by W. R. Stevens.

In the spring of 1921, Day banned dancing for the final weeks of the semester, declaring that "we are close upon examinations and have no time to dance."

Rules for freshmen at the turn of the century included punishments for the carrying of canes before a football game, for singing class songs before upperclassmen had sung, for staying at a sorority after 9:30 P.M., and for smoking on campus.

The first issue of the *Daily Orange* appeared on September 15, 1903. The sixth student newspaper in the university's history, it faced many financial problems in its first years. But the university's purchase of the Orange Publishing Company—which kept down costs by keeping the printing in-house—and the raising of the athletic fee to $2.50, with the consent of the student body, to include a subscription to the *DO*, allowed the newspaper to flourish; it serves as the primary student newspaper to this day.

Front page, first issue of the *Daily Orange*, September 15, 1903.

Voted "Best Looking Man on Campus," 1903.

Dorm life: students living in Winchell Hall, 1908.

Dorm life: student room, 1908.

Hazing of freshmen, ca. 1917.

Daily Orange staff, 1911–12.

Varsity cheerleaders, 1918–19.

School of Architecture, Crouse College, ca. 1920.

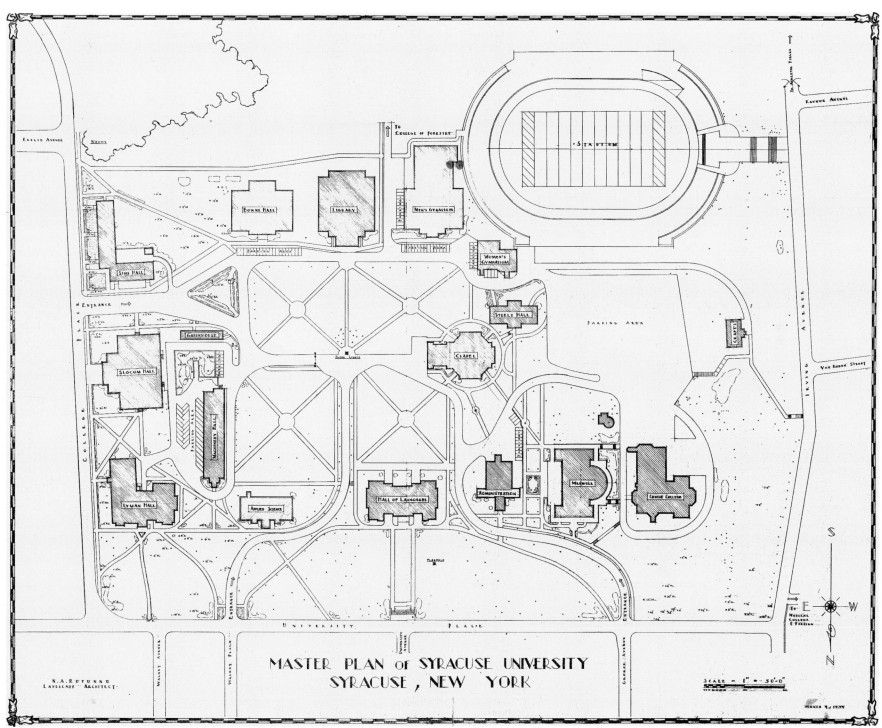

Map of the university, 1939.

Leadership

CHARLES WESLEY FLINT, FALL 1922–1936

The forty-two-year-old Flint, who had previously served as president of Cornell College in Mount Vernon, Iowa, guided Syracuse University through the nation's greatest challenge—the Great Depression. In 1936, he resigned to become the bishop of the Methodist Church in Atlanta.

WILLIAM PRATT GRAHAM, 1936–1942

Graham had lived his entire life in Syracuse and was the first Syracuse alumnus to become chancellor. Graduating in 1889 with a degree in liberal arts, he joined the faculty of his alma mater nine years later, teaching electrical engineering. Graham served as Flint's vice chancellor, and upon Flint's retirement Graham announced that he would serve as chancellor only for a short period of time, "until my successor shall be appointed. . . . I assume that the committee . . . will continue its search for a younger man."

Charles W. Flint.

William P. Graham.

The 1929 log-cutting contest. The event was sponsored annually by the College of Forestry. *Left to right:* Vice Chancellor Graham, Chancellor Flint, Dean Franklin F. Moon, Mayor Charles G. Hanna of Syracuse.

Graham at Women's Day (undated).

Further Growth

Charles Flint inherited a Syracuse University that had expanded beyond the wildest dreams of its founders, but by 1920 was operating in deficit because of the amount of money Day had spent to jumpstart the expansion. Flint not only succeeded in getting rid of Day's deficits but also managed the building of the Maxwell School and Hendricks Chapel—all at a time of national economic depression.

The "Roaring Twenties" brought with it a huge post–World War I glut of applicants to the nation's colleges. Enrollment shot up everywhere; Syracuse was no exception. When Day left in 1922, the institution had 5,600 students; one year later, enrollment stood at 6,422. A downward trend in enrollment occurred during the years of the Great Depression, but it had reversed itself by the late 1930s. The freshman class of 1936 was the largest incoming class in the university's history, and that record was surpassed in the succeeding two years. By 1941, enrollment had increased to a prewar figure of 6,641 students.

"The most difficult educational situation in the United States."

Charles W. Flint, referring to Syracuse University

Tuition in 1940: $375 per year.

With that influx of students came an expansion of the institution's curriculum. In 1919, the School of Business Administration opened its doors, fueled largely by an $80,000 donation from automobile magnate Herbert H. Franklin for a professorial chair in transportation. By 1921 it had grown to the point that it was reorganized into a college, one that would include the School of Journalism, founded in 1934 and housed in Yates Castle.

Reference: Richard Wilson, W. Freeman Galpin, and Oscar T. Barck, Jr. *Syracuse University*. Volume III: *The Critical Years*. Syracuse: Syracuse University Press, 1984.

Chester Randomanski, Editor

Daily Orange, May 1, 1938.

In 1922, George H. Maxwell—an SU alum ('88), patent attorney, and member of the university's board—wrote to Flint professing his desire to fund a chair in American citizenship. The following year, he decided to increase the size of his gift to $500,000 and to fund a school rather than a professorship. The Maxwell School of Citizenship and Public Affairs opened on October 2, 1924. Its first home was the second floor of Slocum Hall; it began with six students. It quickly outgrew its space, and on November 12, 1937, Maxwell Hall

George H. Maxwell.

Former president Herbert C. Hoover, speaking at Maxwell Hall dedication, November 12, 1937.

was dedicated. In the words of its first dean, William E. Mosher, the goal of the school was to teach an "efficient citizenship": a program of studies that would allow the graduate to find a job in government or the public sector.

Maxwell Hall.

Statue of George Washington in Maxwell Hall lobby, sculpted by Jean-Antoine Houdon.

Law School: Ely Apartments (Hackett Hall).

Paul Shipman Andrews.

Harry Ganders (*left*).

Former governor Al Smith, chairman of the Board of Trustees of the College of Forestry, laying the cornerstone for Marshall Hall, December 4, 1931.

Maxwell School library, Maxwell Hall.

In fall 1914, Minnie Trowbridge gave $100,000 toward a new building for the law school, then located in the Crouse mansion in downtown Syracuse. In 1926, the school moved into the Ely Apartments—soon to be renamed Hackett Hall— across the street from the Onondaga County Courthouse. The school's curriculum was also reorganized during that period. Under the tutelage of Dean Paul Shipman Andrews, part-time instructors were phased out, and the casebook method of teaching was introduced.

A 1930 report trumpeted that "more than one-quarter of the graduates of Syracuse University are now engaged in educational service. This is the largest of any of the occupational groups of alumni." As a response, Teachers' College grew in the postwar period, largely owing to the influence of its dean, Harry Ganders. In 1926, the University Hill School opened as a laboratory nursery school; in September 1934, a new, all-university School of Education opened.

In January 1930, New York governor Franklin D. Roosevelt announced that the state budget would include $600,000 for a new building at the State College of Forestry. Named in honor of Louis Marshall, and completed in February 1933, the building also housed the Franklin Moon Library.

Marshall Hall.

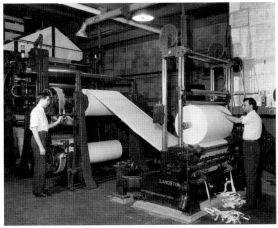

Paper-making machine, billed as the largest of its kind at any American college.

Also in 1933, the building that had been called the Forestry Building was renamed Bray Hall, in honor of the school's first acting dean.

In 1913, Syracuse became the first American university to award a four-year degree in the speech arts. In 1921, it became a part of what many of the period remember as the institution's signature program—the School of Public Speech and Dramatic Art. On May 5, 1931, the school aired its first radio broadcast from the campus; Kenneth Bartlett, then the director of radio, would quickly build a program that was singular in the nation. Also nationally known was the Boar's Head dramatic society and the Tambourine and Bones musical group, both under the guidance of renowned director and instructor Sawyer Falk, who had been appointed head of the Drama Department in 1927.

Kenneth Bartlett and student, 1938.

Sawyer Falk.

Boar's Head production of *Beyond the Horizon*, 1927. In a featured role is future television producer Sheldon Leonard (*far left*).

Not all the arms of the university were growing at the same pace, however. One of Flint's pet projects was to move the medical school from downtown Syracuse up to the main campus. He hoped that this would deal with a problem eloquently stated by the dean of the medical school: "look at the college and you will find more teachers than students." Architect J. Dwight Baum put together the plans for a new medical campus to be located to the south of the new Memorial Hospital and the State Psychiatric Hospital on Crouse Avenue. But the Depression forced Flint to wait. He eventually built the new building with a significant amount of Public Works Administration (PWA) money, yet the building carried almost $1 million in debt upon its completion. On September 29, 1936, the cornerstone of the building was laid by President Franklin Roosevelt; the building was completed in 1937. In 1950, Chancellor William P. Tolley sold the medical school and the Hospital of the Good

Chancellor Graham and President Franklin D. Roosevelt laying the cornerstone of the Medical College.

Left, New Medical College; *right,* Syracuse Memorial Hospital.

Shepherd to the state of New York for a little over $2.5 million.

Many observers in the Roaring Twenties bemoaned the fact that religion seemed to play less of a role in the lives of the nation's youth. Flint struck out at the temper of the times by banning gambling at football games and smoking and drinking on campus. At Syracuse, the chapel seemed to have less of a hold on the community's life in the 1920s than it had had before the war. However, that changed with a significant gift. In 1920, when Senator Francis J. Hendricks died, he left the university a $500,000 gift for a chapel to be built in the name of his wife, Eliza Jane. Construction began in April 1929, and the 1,450-seat chapel was formally dedicated on June 8, 1930.

Construction of Hendricks Chapel, May 1929.

Service in Hendricks Chapel, ca. 1940.

Hendricks Chapel.

Athletics

Football in the late twenties and early thirties
continued to center around the rivalry with
Colgate. For virtually the entire period—from
1924 to 1938—the Orange were winless, with two
ties against the Red Raiders. Then in 1938,
thanks to a fourth-quarter touchdown by Phil
Allen on an end-around, the Orange had their
first victory over Colgate in fourteen years; the
Archbold faithful celebrated by tearing down the
goalposts.

Syracuse Surprises Colgate, 7-0

Orange Snaps 13-Year Jinx On 4th-Period Tally by Allen

Daily Orange report of Colgate game, November 4, 1938.

Of the several outstanding players of the period,
three stand out. Wilmeth Sidat-Singh, one of the
east's leading passers, suffered intense discrimina-
tion; he was black, not a Hindu, as many publici-
ty people maintained. When in 1937 the University of Maryland refused to play Syracuse because
Singh was on their team, he stayed in his hotel
room rather than have the game canceled (the
Orange lost, 13-0). Singh was instrumental in the
thrilling come-from-behind victory over Cornell
in 1938 (19-17). Marty Glickman played with
Singh; his two catches for touchdowns keyed a
14-7 upset of Cornell in 1937. He also starred in
track. During the summer of his sophomore year,
Glickman was denied the right to run in the 1936
Olympic Games, which were held in Berlin,
because he was a Jew. Hugh "Duffy" Daugherty,
who would eventually coach for Michigan State,
was one of the best guards in the east.

Lew Andreas, who coached football and basketball, and who served as the university's athletic
director, called Vic Hanson the greatest athlete in
the university's history. Generally accepted as
one of the greatest ends ever to play the college
game, Hanson captained one of the Hill's greatest
basketball teams. One-third of the "Three

Marty Glickman.

Wilmeth Sidat-Singh.

Vic Hanson.

Orange basketball team, 1925–26, in the *Onondagan*, 1927.

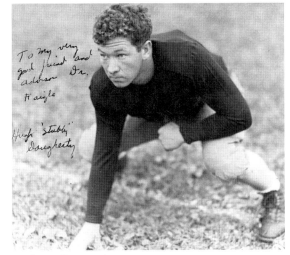

Hugh "Duffy" Daugherty.

"Hanson in Action" (undated).

Musketeers" with Charlie Lee and Gotch Carr, Hanson led the Orange to a 20-1 record in 1925–26 (the only loss coming to Penn State, 37-31), earning a national championship for the university.

Bob Heald runs for the Orangemen against Wisconsin, 1941.

Outstanding Educators

M. Eunice Hilton, dean of women, 1936–49, and director of the innovative Student Dean Program.

Prof. Irene Sargent, History of Fine Arts, 1895–1932.

Student Life

"Syracuse University refuses to confer its degrees upon a student until he has shown the ability to use the English language correctly and easily."

Syracuse University Bulletin, 1927

Prof. Helene W. Hartley, School of Education.

Cheerleaders, 1931.

"Syracuse-in-China." Missionary work for the Methodist Church in the city of Chungking, 1921–43. Photograph by Floyd H. Hopkins.

Annie Louise Macleod, dean of the College of Home Economics.

Dorm life: dormitory double, 1938.

The Building Bulge of William Tolley   1942–1969

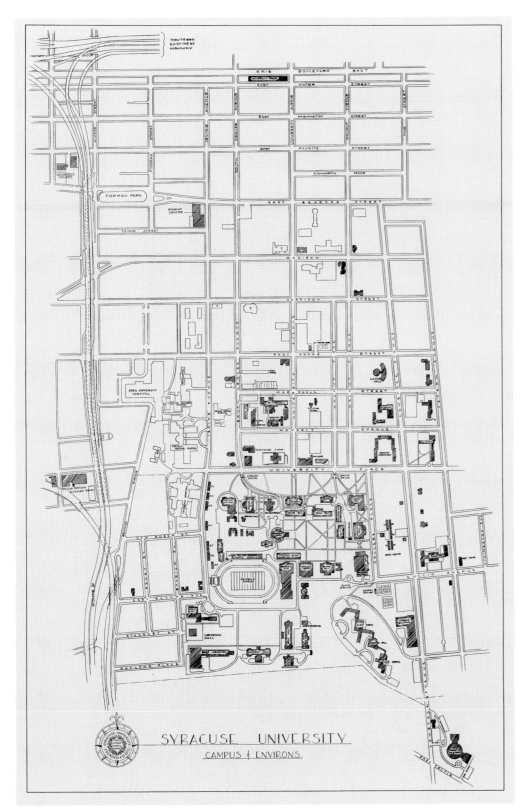

Map of the university, 1968.

Leadership

WILLIAM PEARSON TOLLEY, 1942–1969

A native of Binghamton, New York, Tolley earned a bachelor's (1922) and master's (1924) of arts from Syracuse, as well as a bachelor of divinity from Drew Theological Seminary and a master's and doctoral degree from Columbia University. As president of Allegheny College during the Depression, Tolley guided that struggling institution to fiscal solvency. When he took over the chancellorship at Syracuse in 1942, it was assumed by the board that Tolley could work the same magic on the Hill. He did.

Tolley at fiftieth reunion of Class of 1914, in 1964.

William P. Tolley.

Tolley playing the saxophone.

Tolley at fiftieth reunion of Class of 1922, in 1972.

World War II

The December 7, 1941, devastation at Pearl Harbor plunged the nation into war; the November 1942 decision to extend the draft to all eighteen-year-old males turned many of the nation's universities into *de facto* all-female schools virtually overnight. By the end of 1943, Syracuse University had lost more than a third of its total enrollment. To boost enrollment, Tolley welcomed the presence of military programs on campus—programs such as the Navy's V-12 program, the Army Specialized Training Program, and an Air Force training program that sent close to 2,700 cadets to the university to begin their training. This decision wreaked havoc on a university that at the time had only three dormitories, but thanks to the largely vacated fraternity houses, and Tolley's purchase of nearby Auburn Theological Seminary, the cadets had a place to live.

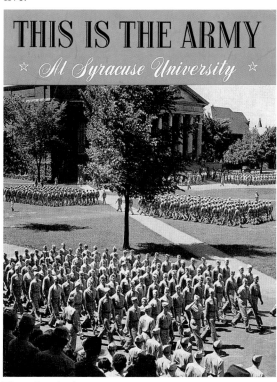

The university in 1944.

Reference: John Robert Greene with Karrie A. Baron. *Syracuse University.* Volume IV: *The Tolley Years, 1942–1969.* Syracuse: Syracuse University Press, 1996.

Cadets in the classroom, ca. 1944.

"I knew we could not survive without students, and that meant men in uniform."

William P. Tolley

Women cadets on campus during World War II. From the *Onondagan,* 1943.

Civilian pilot training program for women, 1943.

Dean Edith Smith, with Evelyn Starr Osborne, 1947.

The war years had a profound effect on the institution's female student body. A nationwide program to enlist women for the war effort on the home front made its way to the Hill. Women signed up for courses in air raid training, mechanics, communications, typing, and home nursing. In 1944, the *Daily Orange* flourished under its first all-female staff. The need for nurses on the foreign fronts sparked a rapid curricular development at Syracuse; thanks to the efforts of Edith H. Smith, then with the National Nursing Council for War Service, the School of Nursing opened in June 1943.

As it was throughout the nation, austerity was the byword on the Hill during the war years. The *Daily Orange* saved paper by appearing four days a week instead of five; many organizations ran war bond drives; and in May 1943, Tolley can-

Bond drives on campus. From the *Onondagan*, 1943.

"Syracusans on the Casualty List," *Alumni News*, November 1945.

celed intercollegiate athletics for the duration of the war. In 1945, the institution not only celebrated its seventy-fifth anniversary but also joined with the entire world in celebrating the end of the war. About 18,000 alumni and former students of Syracuse University served in the war. Of these, 195 were killed, and 51 were listed as missing in action.

The "G.I. Bulge" and the Building Blitz of the 1950s

Everyone expected college enrollment to increase immediately after the war; few were prepared to deal with the stampede of veterans into the classroom. By 1947, enrollment in the nation's universities was already 2.3 million; of that number, half were veterans, most of whom paid for college with the new G.I. Bill. In the four years immediately following the war, enrollment at Syracuse quintupled. Tolley imaginatively solved the resulting lack of space by purchasing 175 trailers from the Navy. These trailers were located in a DeWitt apple orchard near Drumlins Country Club—the area would affectionately become known as "Mud Hollow." Tolley also purchased twenty-five two-family prefabricated housing units from a war-workers colony in Massena; these were located at the northeast corner of the

"Mud Hollow" trailers.

Prefab housing at University Farm (which became Skytop/Slocum Heights).

Veterans' Co-op Food Store.

Quonset huts on main campus.

"Family life": married student housing.

University Farm—now known as Skytop and Slocum Heights. More permanent housing came with the purchase of close to seven hundred Quonset huts. They were located near Morningside Cemetery, on a vacant lot on Colvin Street called Collendale, on the main campus behind Crouse College, and up at Skytop. The sense of community was strong; toward the end of the 1940s, as the veterans left, the university turned the barracks into the institution's first married student housing.

"T-Road."

Hinds Hall.

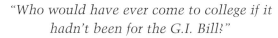

Tolley knew that the wave of the future was in hard scientific research. The fastest growing college in the university during the period was the College of Applied Science—more than 25 percent of the returning veterans asked for engineering training. To house its expansion, Tolley bid on the Naval War Plant on Syracuse's Thompson Road, which had housed General Electric's research facility during the war. The university shared what became known as "T Road" with Carrier Corporation until 1954, when the university sold its interest in the plant for $3.5 million. Engineering students moved back to campus, occupying four two-story barracks at Collendale. In 1955, the first of a projected two-building engineering complex was opened on the main campus. Named for William Hinds of the Crouse-Hinds Corporation, the $940,000 building served some six hundred engineering students.

Engineering was not the only school that thrived in the immediate postwar era. The School of Art developed into a nationally recognized profession-

Joe and Emily Lowe Art Gallery.

al school, noted for innovations such as the Mural Program, where undergraduates worked side-by-side with muralists such as Marion Greenwood. The program was spurred by the construction of the first new building on campus since 1937. A $150,000 gift from businessman Joseph Lowe and his wife, Emily, was the lead gift for the art center that bore their names. Built for $294,000 and dedicated in May 1952, it housed the growing program as well as a series of galleries. Tolley also upgraded the art faculty; his most famous coup was the hiring of Yugoslav freedom fighter and sculptor Ivan Mestrovič.

Marion Greenwood, working on mural in Slocum Hall.

Ivan Mestrovič, with his *Man and Freedom.*

The School of Journalism's strength in print journalism was one of the mainstays of the university—in 1949, the *Daily Orange* had a circulation
of sixteen thousand. The expansion of the
school's offerings in radio and television was a
key curricular development of the 1950s. The
school's radio center had been organized in 1930;
in 1946, the radio workshop was expanded into a
student broadcasting group. Located originally in
the basement of Carnegie Library, the student
station was first known as WORK, and it provided taped shows to local stations. Then in April
1947, SU became the first college in the nation to
have its own low-power FM station, WJIV-FM.
Three months after its first broadcast, the station
changed its name to incorporate the letters of the
journalism honor society, Alpha Epsilon Rho;
thus was WAER born.

Daily Orange staff; in prefab no. 32, 1953.

WAER studio, ca. 1950.

WAER interview with Paul Winchell and Jerry Mahoney.

With the veterans came an increased demand for
evening and extension classes. In 1946, the
School of Extension Teaching was reorganized
into University College (UC). It moved from
offices in the University Block to larger quarters
on the site of the old medical school. Under

University College, Peck Hall.

University College banner, ca. 1940.

Adult class at University College, ca. 1950.

deans Kenneth Bartlett and Alexander Charters,
UC established extension centers throughout
New York State, developed the noncredit
Humanistic Studies Center, and administered
programs as diverse as social work and the
Regent Theater.

An increased enrollment meant an increased need
for new dormitory space—the prefabs simply
were not enough. Between 1952 and 1962, nine
new dormitories were built. The first, Shaw Hall,
opened in September 1952 thanks to a gift from
the estate of Mary Margaret Shaw. It originally
housed 335 women. The generosity of IBM chairman Thomas Watson and university trustee
Frank J. Marion funded a u-shaped complex on
University Place that bore each of their names
and housed 498 men. Construction on "Mount
Olympus"—a tract of land to the south of the
main campus that had been known in the 1930s
as "The Elephant's Back"—yielded two dorms
named after former chancellors: Flint Hall (1956)
and Day Hall (1958). Both dorms originally
housed women—Flint housed 530 and Day
housed 455—all of whom remember walking the
five ramps and seventy-nine steps up the
"Mount" to their rooms. Sadler Hall (1960,

Shaw Hall.

Watson Hall.

Kimmel Hall.

Katharine Sibley at ground breaking for the Women's Building, November 15, 1950.

Flint Hall.

Sadler Hall.

The Women's Building.

Day Hall.

Penny drive for the Women's Building, 1947.

White Hall, 1953.

named after a former Onondaga County judge), DellPlain Hall (1961, named after a university trustee), and Kimmel Hall (1962) rounded out the first stage of main campus dorm construction.

The first donation for a women's building came in 1910, when Cleveland alumni donated ten dol-lars. After that, bake sales, penny drives, and other methods were used to raise money. Ground was finally broken in November 1950, and the building was dedicated on November 17, 1953. Covering one full acre of ground, it had three gymnasiums, a swimming pool, a dance studio, and six bowling alleys.

Construction of a building for the law school, housed in the downtown Hackett Hall since 1926, allowed the school to move to the main campus for the first time in its history. Named after a Syracuse lawyer and the president of the *Syracuse Post-Standard*, and costing $922,000, the Ernest I. White building was dedicated on

Arnold Grant, at dedication of Grant Auditorium, April 28, 1967.

At dedication of HBC, October 22, 1962. *Left to right:* Chancellor Tolley; John Tuttle, board chairman of the Crouse-Hinds Foundation; and Mrs. Huntington B. Crouse.

Chancellor Tolley and President Johnson, August 5, 1964.

December 11, 1954. In 1967, a new auditorium, named after board member Arnold Grant, was added to White Hall.

One building project was testimony to the growth of the College of Liberal Arts. Huntington Beard Crouse Hall—quickly dubbed "HBC"—was named for a former trustee and dedicated on October 22, 1962. It housed seventy-seven offices, two auditoriums, language labs, and a cartography and photography studio. The $1.6 million structure was also the first fully air-conditioned building on campus.

The second phase of Tolley's "building bulge" began in the spring of 1961, when he announced that the university had committed itself to raising $76 million by 1970—the year of the institution's one-hundredth anniversary. One of the largest gifts was used to expand the growing School of Journalism, which since 1953 had had its office in the Women's Gymnasium. Publishing magnate Samuel I. Newhouse pledged $1 million toward the building of a new school of journalism. In July 1962, he increased his pledge by $15 million and the project was expanded to reflect

the construction of three projected buildings: the Samuel I. Newhouse Communications Center at Syracuse University. Designed by renowned architect I. M. Pei, the first building—"Newhouse I"—won several prestigious honors for its innovative design. Newhouse I was dedicated on August 5, 1964, a day highlighted not only by the presence of President Lyndon B. Johnson as the dedication speaker, but also by Johnson's use of that speech to announce the deployment of Air Force strikes against North Vietnam as a response to alleged bombing of American ships in the Gulf of Tonkin.

The second phase of the building bulge also led to the construction of two more dormitories: Booth Hall (1963), which was named for a university trustee, and Lawrinson Hall (1965), a twenty-one-story structure that at the time was the second-tallest skyscraper in the city of Syracuse.

Huntington Beard Crouse Hall.

S. I. Newhouse and building plans.

Newhouse I.

Booth Hall.

Lawrinson Hall.

Athletics

The 1943 football season was canceled owing to the war, and in the late forties the team had several mediocre seasons. One glowing spot, however, was the play of Bernie Custis, the nation's first black college starting quarterback. Dubbed "The Arm" in the Syracuse press, Custis's talents were lost in a 1-8 season in 1948; the next season, however, Custis passed for 1,121 yards—a new school record.

All sports were affected by a devastating fire on January 12, 1947, which destroyed Archbold Gymnasium. The largest fire in the university's history, it resulted in a loss estimated at $2 million. All sports teams had to scramble to find locker and practice facilities until the gymnasium reopened in 1948; renovations would not be complete until three years later.

Floyd "Ben" Schwartzwalder's first season on the Hill was 1949; the Orange went 4-5—but they beat Colgate, 35-7. It was a harbinger of things to come. Schwartzwalder—a native of West Virginia,

Archbold Gymnasium fire, January 12, 1947.

officer in the Eighty-Second Airborne during World War II, and former coach at Muhlenberg College—would serve as head football coach on the Hill for twenty-five years. In that period, his teams went to seven bowl games, won four Lambert Trophies (best collegiate team in the east), and had twenty-two straight winning seasons and one national championship.

The addition of two remarkable running backs was key to Schwartzwalder's success at the end of the 1950s. Schwartzwalder remembered Jim Brown's "indestructibility"; the straight-ahead

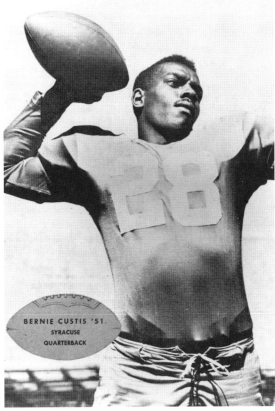

Bernie Custis.

Ben Schwartzwalder.

Jim Brown, 1955.

Ernie Davis.

Ernie Davis's performance won him the game's "Outstanding Back" award.

Schwartzwalder and players with National Championship Trophy, 1960.

power of the "Manhasset Mauler" took the Orange to the 1957 Cotton Bowl, where, despite being overmatched and facing many acts of racial taunting, the Orange lost by only one point, 28-27. Brown had taken the number 44 on his jersey because no one else wanted it. His successor in the backfield would inherit that now-storied number. Where Brown ran over the opposition, Ernie Davis danced around it. Only a sophomore in 1959, Davis would lead the Orange to their only national championship to date.

The 1959 football season was the most storied in the history of SU sports. After becoming the last victim in the Orangemen's undefeated regular season, UCLA coach Billy Barnes proclaimed Schwartzwalder's team "one of the greatest teams

I have ever seen." The January 1960 Cotton Bowl game against the University of Texas bears out Barnes's assessment. Davis was the star of the game, catching an eighty-seven-yard touchdown pass and intercepting a Texas pass in the third quarter, which led to a touchdown. The final score: Texas 14, the national champion Syracuse University Orangemen, 23. Schwartzwalder went on to win coach of the year honors. Two years later, Davis won the Heisman Trophy and was drafted by the Cleveland Browns; on May 18, 1963, he died from an advanced case of leukemia.

For SU, 1959 was also a championship year in another sport. In 1949, Coach Ned Ten Eyck had retired as the coach of Syracuse crew. For several years, there were few winning seasons. In 1955, Loren Schoel was named the new coach, and the luck of the "Syracuse Navy" soon changed. In 1959, Syracuse beat out the crew of the Naval Academy by one and one-tenth of a second, and

The 1960 Onondagan . . .

. . . told the tale of the 1960 Cotton Bowl victory.

February 6, 1968: A new committee on Undergraduate Student Life decides to permit drinking at registered functions.

February 6–7, 1968: The Outfit for Unorthodox Teaching sponsors an "All-Night Teach-Out" in Hendricks Chapel. The organization begins to publicize its plans for a "Free University"—one that would be both student-operated and tuition-free.

February–March 1968: A series of sit-ins at the university protests the actions of Dow Chemical Company—the chief manufacturer of napalm—and its continued recruitment of prospective employees through the university's placement service. Several students arrested in the protests are placed on disciplinary probation for "an indefinite period" by an administrative disciplinary body.

Student protest of Dow Chemical Company, 1968.

March 12, 1968: On one of the most vocal days of the Dow protests, the university announces its plans to configure a coeducational dormitory.

April 4, 1968: King is assassinated in Memphis, Tennessee.

April 19, 1968: Chuck Hicks is elected president of the student body.

May 1968: Tolley announces his retirement, to become effective in September 1969.

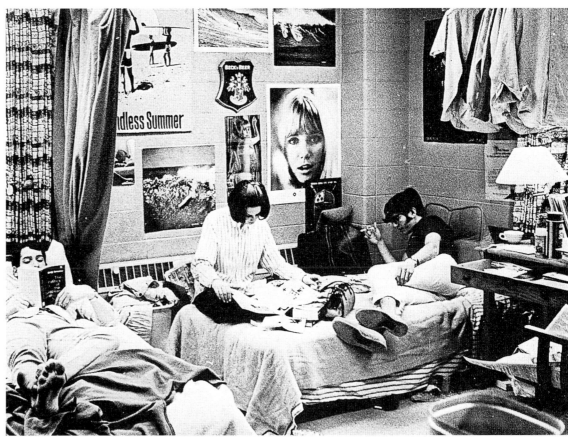

Coed dormitory life, from the *Onondagan*, 1969.

Chuck Hicks (*left*) with John Diamond.

Tolley's retirement party, 1969.

June 6, 1968: Sen. Robert F. Kennedy is assassinated in Los Angeles, California.

August 26–29, 1968: The Democratic National Convention in Chicago is interrupted by several days of rioting in the streets; many Syracuse University students are in attendance.

October 15, 1968: Between six and ten thousand people from the university area join in a candlelight march; it is part of the events of the fall National Mobilization Against the War.

October 29, 1968: Republican presidential candidate Richard M. Nixon visits the Onondaga County War Memorial in Syracuse; several protesters from Syracuse University interrupt his speech by singing "The Sounds of Silence."

November 1968: Nixon defeats Democrat Hubert H. Humphrey and third-party candidate George Wallace for the presidency.

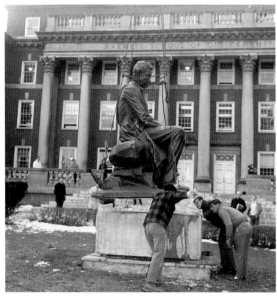

Installation of Fraser statue of Lincoln.

December 6, 1968: Sculptor James Earle Fraser's cast of Abraham Lincoln is installed in the courtyard of the Maxwell School.

March 14, 1969: After their request to meet with Tolley is spurned, a group of 150 students calling themselves the United Black Students demonstrates outside the Administration Building. Several of their demands are agreed to by the administration, including the creation of the Afro-American Cultural Center and a thousand-volume Martin Luther King, Jr., Memorial Library Collection.

Corbally introduced to campus at Maxwell Auditorium, March 25, 1969 (Corbally, *far left*, is shaking hands with Michael O. Sawyer, a Maxwell faculty member; Chancellor Tolley is to Corbally's immediate left).

March 25, 1969: Chancellor-elect John Corbally is introduced to the faculty at Maxwell Auditorium.

"A university should remain an open institution so no one has to tear the place apart to be heard."

John Corbally, March 25, 1969

George Arents Pioneer Medal

Honorary Degrees and Commencement Speakers

Institutions, as well as people, are known by the company they keep...

Marian Anderson, 1960.

William F. Buckley, Jr., 1969.

Kurt Vonnegut, 1994.

Ralph Bunche, 1949.

Hubert Humphrey, 1965.

Daniel Patrick Moynihan, 1969.

Donna Shalala, 1995.

Sen. John F. Kennedy, 1957.

Nelson Rockefeller, 1967.

Julian Bond, 1970.

Robert Fulghum, 1998.

Earl Warren, 1960.

Walter Cronkite, 1968.

Sen. Edward M. Kennedy, 1973.

Other Honored Guests

Harry S Truman, May 1960.

Daniel Ellsberg and G. Gordon Liddy, 1981.

Elie Wiesel, 1988.

Robert Frost, April 1959.

Robert F. Kennedy, February 1965.

Rev. Jesse Jackson, 1984.

Gov. Bill Clinton campaigning on the quad, April 6, 1992.

Bob Hope with Bruce Riedel, the Saltine Warrior, April 1966.

Leonard Nimoy, 1984.

Hillary Clinton, April 1994.

Aaron Copland, conducting a rehearsal of the Syracuse University Orchestra, 1975.

Dr. Benjamin Spock, 1986.

Jerry Springer, January 1995.

The George Arents Pioneer Medal

"Every year Columbia University gives five medals, restricted to the alumni of the university, for some distinguished thing done. It tends to bind the alumni of Columbia. . . . It strikes me that it might be a goodly thing for this university to do the same thing."

George Arents, then–vice president of the Board of Trustees, at board meeting, June 3, 1938.

George Arents. Painting by Frank O. Salisbury, 1930.

Mrs. Huntington B. (Florence) Crouse, *(center)*, 1950.

Eric Faigle *(right)* with Gordon Hoople, 1959.

Sheldon Leonard *(center)*, with Kenneth G. Bartlett *(left)* and Chancellor Tolley, 1967.

Left to right: Robert B. Menschel, Chester Soling, Lora S. Flanagan, James A. Britton, 1980.

Douglas Barclay, 1984.

Left to right: Richard Hayden, Betsey Johnson, Dick Stockton, Sen. Alfonse D'Amato, 1985.

Michael O. Sawyer, 1986.

Steve Kroft, 1992.

Dave Bing with Chancellor Shaw, 1994.

Vanessa Williams with Chancellor Shaw, 1996.

William Safire with Chancellor Shaw, 1997.

Marty Glickman with Michael Somich *(left)* and Chancellor Shaw, 1998.

> *"Our very own jewels."*
>
> Lansing G. Baker, senior vice president, University Relations, on the Arents Medal winners

GEORGE ARENTS PIONEER MEDAL WINNERS

1939
William M. Smallwood
Dorothy C. Thompson
John S. Young

1940
Frank J. O'Neill
Anna V. Rice
Herman G. Weiskotten

1941
Lurelle V. Guild
Cecilia B. Martin
J. Robert Rubin

1942
Cora D. Graham
William P. Graham

1943
Carl L. Bausch
DeWitt T. MacKenzie
Marguerite W. Wriston

1944
J. Winifred Hughes
Edmund H. Lewis

1945
Neal Brewster
Ernest H. Hawkins
Katharine Sibley

1946
J. Roscoe Drummond
Winifred Fisher

1947
T. Aaron Levy
Harry L. Upperman

1948
LeGrande A. Diller
Welthy H. Fisher
Drew Middleton

1949
Hilda G. Taylor
Harry E. Weston
Nelia G. White

1950
Harry J. Carman
Clara B. Congdon
Florence B. Crouse

1951
T. Frank Dolan
Helene W. Hartley
Gordon D. Hoople

1952
Evelyn M. Duvall
Edgar B. Ingraham
William D. Lewis

1953
Mary A. Becker
Martha K. Phillips
Carleton F. Sharpe

1954
Gertrude S. Brooks
Edward C. Reifenstein
William P. Tolley

1955
Leslie A. Bryan
June Buchanan
Malcolm P. Ferguson

1956
Florence K. Murray
D. Kenneth Sargent
Clarence L. Van Schaick

1957
Walter S. Bourlier
Pyo Wook Han
Agnes E. Law

1958
Darius A. Davis
Elizabeth S. Herbert
Lester O. Schriver

1959
Vernon L. deTar
Eric H. Faigle
Clare B. Williams

1960
Donald Q. Faragher
J. Burch McMorran
Eloise A. Woolever

1961
William G. Atwell
Harvey O. Banks
Marion C. Link

1962
Margaret L. Arnold
Norris O. Johnson
Eric W. Will

1963
Lewis P. Andreas
Mary Caroline Egan
Frederick G. Vosburgh

1964
Frances Clark Dietzold
Dr. Samuel Rosen

1965
Donald Jay Grout
Dr. J. G. Fred Hiss

1966
James F. Bunting
Helen R. Hagan
Millard G. Roberts

1967
Jean DuBois Galkin
Sheldon Leonard
Joseph H. Murphy

1968
Robert W. Cutler
Delmont K. Pfeffer
Dr. Madeline J. Thornton

1969
Franklyn S. Barry
Donald S. MacNaughton
Cornelia T. Snell

1970
Louis R. Bruce
Julie Chase Fuller
John A. Olver

1971
Martine Burdick Clayton
John D. MacDonald
Bernard M. Singer

1972
Elizabeth Barstow Alton
Albert W. Brown
Kenneth E. Buhrmaster

1973
Arthur J. Barry
Marjorie R. Elliott
Howard F. Miller

1974
Phyllis Hickman Demong
Raymond T. Schuler
Demetria M. Taylor

1975
Horace J. Landry
Rosemary S. Nesbitt
Lawrence R. White

1976
Floyd D. Little
Nancy Harvey Steorts
Lee J. Topp

1977
Harry A. and Dorothy Wende Devlin
Susan Reid Greene
Gerald J. Leider

1978
Robert W. Cornell
Seymour M. Leslie
L. Douglas Meredith
Dorothy E. Rowe

1979
Louis F. Bantle
Charles E. Boddie
Gerald Stiller

1980
James A. Britton
Lora S. Flanagan
Robert B. Menschel
Chester Soling

1981
Marcus A. Clements
Carlisle S. Floyd, Jr.
Athena C. Kouray
Christian X. Kouray

1982
Dr. P. Gordon Gould
Eva Holmes Lee
Dr. George A. Sisson
Lewis Slingerland

1983
Stella Biercuk Blum
William J. Brodsky
Sidney L. Krawitz
Hon. Tarky J. Lombardi

1984
H. Douglas Barclay
Mel Elfin
Robert Pietrafesa
Maxine B. Singer

1985
Sen. Alfonse D'Amato
Richard S. Hayden
Betsey Johnson
Dick Stockton

1986
Robert A. Beck
Vincent H. Cohen
Michael O. Sawyer

1987
George H. Babikian
Robin R. Burns
Anthony C. Chevins
William J. Smith

1988
Candace Bahouth
Douglas D. Danforth
Robert S. Phillips
Peter W. Yenawine

1989
H. Peter Guber
Luise Meyers Kaish
John L. Martin

1990
Diane Camper
Theresa Howard-Carter
Eleanor A. Ludwig
Albert Murray
Richard C. Pietrafesa

1991
L. Ross Love
Joan Lines Oates
J. Robert Tomlinson

1992
Steve Kroft
Susan C. Penny
Robert S. Rigolosi
Anthony Y. C. Yeh

1993
George W. Campbell, Jr.
Mary Schmidt Campbell
John A. Couri
Marvin K. Lender

1994
Martin N. Bandier
David Bing
JoAnn Heffernan Heisen

1995
Dick Clark

1996
Lt. Col. Eileen M. Collins
Ruth Johnson Colvin
Marshall Gelfand
Vanessa L. Williams

1997
Irma Ginsberg Kalish
F. Story Musgrave
Arthur Rock
William Safire

1998
M. Elizabeth Carnegie
David Falk
Marty Glickman
Alan Rafkin

1999
Lynn Ahrens
Bradley J. Anderson
Molly Corbett Broad
Bernie Wohl

2000
Renée Schine Crown
Antje B. Lemke
Charles V. Willie

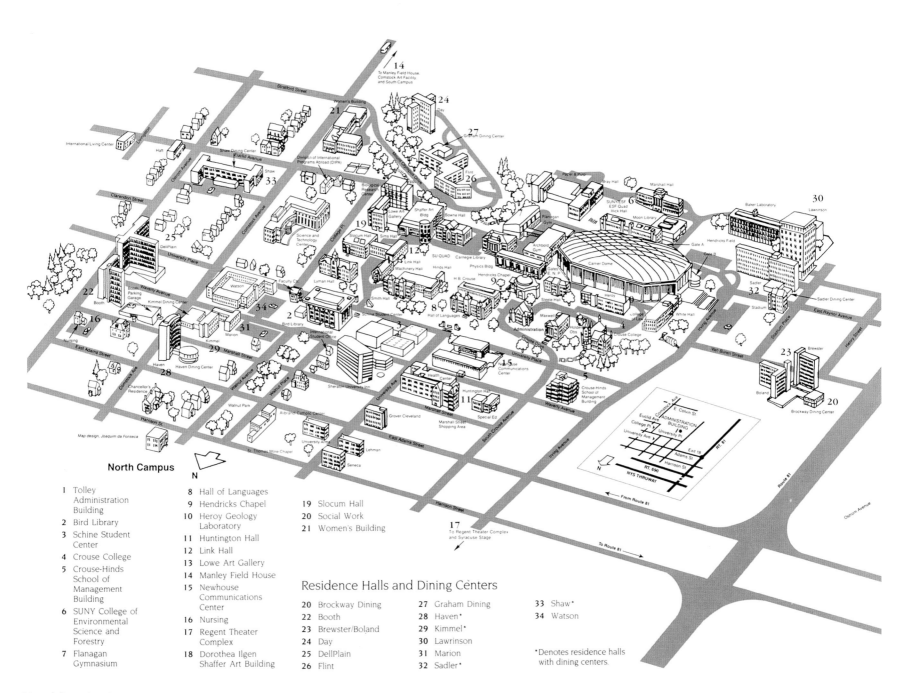

North Campus

1 Tolley Administration Building
2 Bird Library
3 Schine Student Center
4 Crouse College
5 Crouse-Hinds School of Management Building
6 SUNY College of Environmental Science and Forestry
7 Flanagan Gymnasium
8 Hall of Languages
9 Hendricks Chapel
10 Heroy Geology Laboratory
11 Huntington Hall
12 Link Hall
13 Lowe Art Gallery
14 Manley Field House
15 Newhouse Communications Center
16 Nursing
17 Regent Theater Complex
18 Dorothea Ilgen Shaffer Art Building
19 Slocum Hall
20 Social Work
21 Women's Building

Residence Halls and Dining Centers

20 Brockway Dining
22 Booth
23 Brewster/Boland
24 Day
25 DellPlain
26 Flint
27 Graham Dining
28 Haven*
29 Kimmel*
30 Lawrinson
31 Marion
32 Sadler*
33 Shaw*
34 Watson

*Denotes residence halls with dining centers.

Map of the university, 1990.

Leadership

JOHN E. CORBALLY, JR., 1969–1971

A veteran of World War II, Corbally earned his bachelor's (1947) and master's (1950) degrees at the University of Washington, and his doctorate in educational administration and finance (1955) from the University of California, Berkeley. Corbally served as director of the personnel budget, executive assistant to the president, and vice president for administration at Ohio State University from 1955 to 1969. After his brief tenure at Syracuse University, Corbally became the head of the Illinois State University system.

MELVIN A. EGGERS, 1971–1991

Born in Fort Wayne, Indiana, in 1916, Eggers worked part-time at a dairy and a bank to earn money for tuition at the Bloomington campus of Indiana University. There he earned his bachelor's in economics in 1940; the next year he received his master's. During World War II, Eggers worked as a Japanese language translator; following the war, he earned his doctorate at Yale University (1950). That same year, he came to the Maxwell School as a member of the Economics Department. Ten years later, he was named chair of that department. He served as chairman of the University Senate's Agenda Committee, and as Corbally's vice chancellor for academic affairs, before becoming acting chancellor upon Corbally's resignation in 1971.

> *"I was reminded of the many gifts Mel Eggers gave to Syracuse. He was unstinting in lending his heart, soul, and intellect to this institution."*
>
> Chancellor Kenneth Shaw

John E. Corbally.

Melvin A. Eggers.

Corbally with student, 1969.

Eggers at commencement, 1972.

Eggers and student.

The Turn of the Decade and Student Activism

The year of 1969–70 was to feature the celebration of the university's centennial. Instead, the year will be remembered for student protests exploding on campus—against the war in Vietnam, the university's solicitation of research contracts with the military, and the presence of ROTC on campus. Student leader David Ifshin was largely responsible for organizing the student body.

David Ifshin.

On April 30, 1970—the day of Corbally's formal inauguration ceremonies—President Richard Nixon told the nation that he had widened the Vietnam War by invading Cambodia. During a May 4 protest of his decision, four students were killed at Kent State University in Ohio. After hearing of the news that evening, the "Strike Committee of the May 4 Coalition" declared that Syracuse University was to be shut down. Barricades made out of chicken wire, garbage cans, and other refuse went up that evening. Despite the tension on campus, and the May 7

Reference: John Robert Greene with Karrie A. Baron, Debora D. Hall, and Matthew Sharp. *Syracuse University.* Volume V: *The Eggers Years.* Syracuse: Syracuse University Press, 1998.

takeover of the Administration Building by African-American students, the student strike at Syracuse University was notable for its lack of violence. By May 11, the strike was over; it had cost the university approximately $423,000.

Student strike, May 1970.

Student strike, May 1970.

"I knew that there were going to be problems."

Chancellor John Corbally,
following the killings at Kent State

The May strike coincided with another walkout, one that would have even longer-lasting implications. In the spring, 1970, nine black football players who protested their unexplained benching the previous season, refused to attend spring practice. Despite Corbally's attempts to mediate the situation, the players sat out the entire 1970 season. A twelve-member investigating committee

later found evidence of racism in the football program, and concluded that there was "substance" to the athletes' charges. At the end of the 1973 season, head football coach Ben Schwartzwalder retired.

Football players, spring game, 1969. *Standing, left to right:* Tom Smith, Dwayne Walker, Alif Muhammad (Al Newton), Clarence "Bucky" McGill; *kneeling, left to right:* John Lobon, Dana Harrell, Greg Allen, John Godbolt. Smith graduated before the 1970 boycott; all others pictured participated in the strike. Photograph courtesy John Lobon.

"This was a football issue. That's what people had to understand. . . . The issue was, were the best being played? We said no."

John Lobon, one of the striking football players

Building

Mel Eggers came into the chancellor's chair at a time of almost unprecedented upheaval on campus. Yet his first challenges were financial. Corbally had begun to rebuild and modernize the institution's finances after years of expansion under Tolley. Nevertheless, Eggers inherited a huge cash flow deficit and a massive capital debt. Through a variety of methods, Eggers led the institution toward fiscal recovery by the end of the decade.

He then moved toward a dual program for continuing Tolley's physical expansion of the university. First, Eggers completed the buildings that were

Link Hall.

Ernest S. Bird Library.

William B. Heroy Geology Laboratory.

Bird Library, interior, 1981.

begun under Tolley. Link Hall, the second of a two-building engineering complex, had been dedicated in 1970. The William B. Heroy Geology Laboratory was dedicated in October 1972. Next, finished at a final cost of $13 million, was the Ernest S. Bird Library. Indeed, it cost $100,000 to move three million books and assorted periodicals, microforms, and manuscripts from Carnegie Library and other repositories on campus to the new seven-floor library, which was dedicated on April 6, 1973.

The second phase of Eggers's early program dealt with maintenance to existing buildings that had been deferred for more than a decade. In fall 1971, both Crouse College and Steele Hall were refurbished and repaired. But the most important

phase of this program was the complete renovation of the Hall of Languages, undertaken largely thanks to government grants that became available when HL was placed on the National Register of Historic Places. The renovation, dedicated to popular professor Eric Faigle, began in May 1977; the renewed HL was rededicated on September 6, 1979.

Eggers was then able to move with his own plans for campus expansion. Next to the Carrier Dome, the most ambitious project of Eggers's first decade was the Skytop Housing and Office Complex. Constructed by the Pyramid Corporation, the Skytop project combined new residence centers with a new administrative center. Phase I of Skytop, completed in April 1972, consisted of 260

two-bedroom townhouse apartments. Phase II, completed one year later, opened 63 new buildings that contained 504 new apartments.

As the university's enrollment continued to increase throughout the late 1960s and early 1970s, Eggers strengthened several schools and programs that were strong undergraduate draws. In fall 1971, as part of a major reorganization of the university's academic structure, the Samuel I. Newhouse School of Public Communications was announced. The new school combined the print focus of the old School of Journalism with the Department of Television-Radio. The second building in Sam Newhouse's $15 million pledge was built to house the broadcast side of the new school. Some 5000 square feet larger than the first

Interior renovation of Hall of Languages, 1978.

Exterior renovation of Hall of Languages, 1979.

building, Newhouse II featured teleproduction laboratories that were state-of-the-art. It was dedicated on May 31, 1974, with CBS chairman William S. Paley as the featured speaker and NBC News anchor David Brinkley acting as the master of ceremonies.

Eggers also moved to consolidate and strengthen the university's offerings in the arts and in business. Eggers joined the Schools of Art and Music with the Departments of Speech and Dramatic

Family living at Skytop, 1979.

David Brinkley at Newhouse II dedication dinner, May 31, 1974.

Left to right: William Paley, Mrs. Mitzi Newhouse, and Samuel I. Newhouse at Newhouse II dedication ceremonies, May 31, 1974.

The Samuel I. Newhouse Communications Center at Syracuse University.

L. Richard Oliker (*left*) dean of the School of Management, and Chris J. Witting, chairman of the Syracuse University Board of Trustees, at dedication of Crouse-Hinds School of Management Building, March 22, 1983.

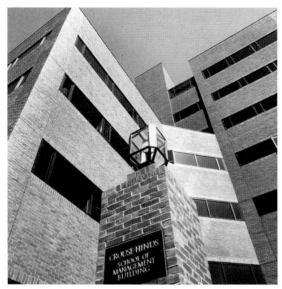

Crouse-Hinds School of Management Building.

Demolition of Archbold Stadium, December 29, 1978.

Raising the roof on the Dome, July 1980.

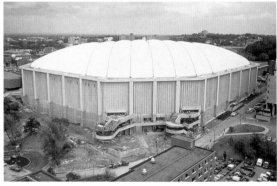

Construction of the Carrier Dome, October 1979.

Carrier Dome.

Arts; thus was born the College of Visual and Performing Arts. The burgeoning School of Management (enrollments in the school had doubled between 1972 and 1978) was aided by a $2.5 million naming gift for a building from the Crouse-Hinds Corporation; in January 1983, the school occupied the eight-story Crouse-Hinds School of Management Building.

By 1969, venerable Archbold Stadium was crumbling. After a protracted period of negotiation with Onondaga County, several aborted plans, and pressure from neighbors who were upset that a new stadium might be built in the Skytop area, Eggers decided to build the new stadium right on top of the old one. The state of New York gave $10 million; the university raised the rest. A $2.75 million donation from the Carrier Corporation served as the naming gift for the

Early rendering of "SU Stadium," ca. 1977.

new stadium, despite the protests of many students and alumni who wanted to see it named the Ernie Davis Dome.

"We must give up Archbold, or give up football. It is as simple as that."

Chancellor Eggers to an alum

The Dome stands with the Hall of Languages and Crouse College as one of the three most recognizable buildings on the Syracuse University campus. Archbold was demolished in the winter of 1978–79; in April 1979, the first concrete footers were poured for construction. Efforts were slowed by a challenge over an environmental impact statement, as well as concerns over minority hiring on the project. Nevertheless, the facility was completed on August 29, 1980, at a final cost of $26.85 million. Even though it occupies 10,000 fewer square feet of space than did Archbold, the inflated fiberglass roof covers 6.5 acres. Not only was it to be used for football and basketball

games, but concerts and professional sporting events were held in the Dome, sparking a protracted battle with the city of Syracuse over the tax assessment of the building.

Eggers had originally wanted an on-campus hotel to be part of a complex that included the Carrier Dome. In spring 1982 he got his wish, as the university negotiated a lease deal with University Avenue Properties, Inc. Students were incensed at a project that necessitated the demolition of several buildings that held student offices (many wore buttons saying "Move it, Mel!"). Nevertheless, on March 20, 1985, the Sheraton University Inn and Conference Center, built at a cost of $19.8 million, was dedicated.

Eggers had also wanted a student center as part of his dream Dome-hotel complex. He was far from the first to call for a new student center; the *Daily Orange* had demanded such a facility in 1911. But it didn't happen until 1982, when Renée Schine Crown, a Syracuse alumna, donated $2.5 million toward its construction. A building

Sheraton University Inn and Conference Center.

Left to right: Edward Larabee Barnes, Renée Schine Crown, and Tarky Lombardi, with original model of the Schine Student Center.

Gov. Mario Cuomo, signing bill enabling funding for the Center for Science and Technology.

Demolition of Winchell Hall (future site of the Schine Student Center), 1984.

Center for Science and Technology.

Dedication of the Schine Student Center, October 18, 1985. *Left to right:* Richard Schine, G. David Schine, Doris Schine Maxwell, Renée Schine Crown, Hildegarde Schine, Chancellor Eggers.

The Hildegarde and J. Myer Schine Student Center.

campaign, chaired by Crown and State Senator Tarky Lombardi, eventually netted $15 million. Dedicated on October 18, 1985, the Hildegarde and J. Myer Schine Student Center would house student government offices, a student-run nightclub called the Milky Way, and a 256-seat dining facility. At the dedication ceremony, the student representative declared, "It exceeds all of our dreams and expectations."

One of the major academic stories of the 1980s was the university's decision to return to hard research, which it had downplayed for two decades, largely as a result of mounting costs and the howls of protests hurled at the university's plethora of government contracts during the war in Vietnam. In February 1984, the CASE Center, a sixteen-institution consortium that focused on computer-enhanced reasoning and computer research, was established. In 1986, the university secured a $27 million loan from the state's Urban Development Corporation; this grant would be the basis for the building of the Center for

Science and Technology, dedicated on March 2, 1989. The largest building ever erected by the university—situated on a five-acre lot—Sci-Tech housed the CASE Center and educational facilities in computer science, electrical and computer engineering, information studies, and chemistry.

With the establishment of the CASE Center and the construction of Sci-Tech, Eggers felt that "the tier of excellence toward which Dr. Tolley directed us has been substantially achieved. But Syracuse University cannot stand still." In November 1987, Eggers announced the $100 million Campaign for Syracuse; by September, 1989—one year ahead of schedule—the university had surpassed that goal. Many gifts to that campaign funded the final phase of Eggers's physical expansion of the university. The Lora

Chancellor Eggers with Dorothea Shaffer, 1977.

Lora and Alfred Flanagan.

South Africa protest, April 23, 1985.

and Alfred Flanagan Gymnasium was completed in October 1989 at a cost of $5.8 million. A $1 million naming gift from Maryland real estate broker Paul Greenberg allowed the university to purchase a house that would become its base of operations in Washington, D.C., when

it opened in March 1990. The $3.25 million gift of Dorothea Ilgen Shaffer and her husband, Maurice Shaffer, funded the Shaffer Art Building, which was dedicated on October 20, 1990. The Ann and Alfred Goldstein Student Center, built in the Skytop complex, was completed

at a cost of $7 million and dedicated on November 9, 1990.

Despite the prevalence of stories about student apathy in the Reagan era, campus activism hardly died in the eighties. One of the biggest causes to

Shaffer Art Building.

Flanagan Gym.

South Africa protest.

Greenberg House.

Goldstein Student Center.

take root around the nation was the protest against college and university investments in South Africa, a nation whose society was structured in the racist system of apartheid. In April 1985, students from a group called the Coalition Against Racism and Apartheid hammered homemade crosses into the ground around the Administration Building and built a tent encampment on the lawn. That summer, the university divested itself of part of its holdings in South Africa, but the protests continued; the following year, a shanty house encampment was built.

On December 21, 1988, a Boeing 747, traveling to New York City from London's Heathrow Airport, exploded only a few moments after takeoff. All 259 people aboard Pan Am 103, including thirty-five Syracuse University students, were killed in what was later determined to be an act of international terrorism. The grieving university held several memorial services, including one at the Carrier Dome; set up a scholarship program in memory of the slain students; and built a plaza at

Memorial service for Pan Am victims, Hendricks Chapel, December 21, 1988.

New York governor Mario Cuomo, Syracuse mayor Tom Young, and Chancellor Eggers at Carrier Dome service for Pan Am victims, January 18, 1989.

The Place of Remembrance.

the main entrance to the campus—the Place of Remembrance.

SU STUDENTS LOST IN THE DOWNING OF PAN AM FLIGHT 103, DECEMBER 21, 1988

Steven Russell Berrell, Fargo, N.D.
Kenneth J. Bissett, Hartsdale, N.Y.
Stephen J. Boland, Nashua, N.H.
Nicole Elise Boulanger, Shrewsbury, Mass.
Timothy M. Cardwell, Cresco, Pa.
Theodora Cohen, Port Jervis, N.Y.
Eric M. Coker, Mendham, N.J.
Jason M. Coker, Mendham, N.J.
Gary L. Colasanti, Melrose, Mass.
Scott Marsh Cory, Old Lyme Court, Conn.
Gretchen Joyce Dater, Ramsey, N.J.
Shannon Davis, Shelton, Conn.
Turhan Michael Ergin, West Hartford, Conn.
John P. Flynn, Montville, N.J.
Pamela Elaine Herbert, Battle Creek, Mich.
Karen Lee Hunt, Webster, N.Y.
Christopher Andrew Jones, Claverack, N.Y.
Julianne F. Kelly, Dedham, Mass.
Wendy A. Lincoln, North Adams, Mass.
Alexander Lowenstein, Morristown, N.J.
Suzanne Marie Miazga, Marcy, N.Y.
Richard Paul Monetti, Cherry Hill, N.J.
Anne Lindsey Otenasek, Baltimore, Md.
Peter R. Peirce, Perrysburg, Ohio.
Sarah S. B. Philipps, Newtonville, Mass.
Frederick "Sandy" Phillips, Little Rock, Ark.
Louise "Luann" Rogers, Olney, Md.
Amy Elizabeth Shapiro, Stamford, Conn.
Thomas Britton Schultz, Ridgefield, Conn.
Cynthia J. Smith, Milton, Mass.
Mark Lawrence Tobin, North Hempstead, N.Y.
Alexia Kathryn Tsairis, Franklin Lakes, N.J.
Nicholas Andreas Vrenios, Washington, D.C.
Kesha Weedon, Bronx, N.Y.
Miriam Luby Wolfe, Severna Park, Md.

Athletics

The 1968 resignation of Fred Lewis as basketball coach on the Hill, and the promotion of his assistant, Roy Danforth, opened a new era. In seven seasons at the helm, Danforth took the team to two NIT tournaments and four appearances in the NCAAs. His teams emphasized speed over power; they had to—their general lack of size led them to be dubbed "Roy's Runts," both in the press and in the hearts of the fans who jammed shoulder-tight in the Manley Field House "zoo." The early seventies were dominated by the play of Dennis DuVal; at the end of his career, "Sweet D" had 1,501 points, second only to Dave Bing in the SU records.

It was, however, the 1974–75 season that brought euphoria to the Hill. Stepping up to fill the shoes of DuVal, Jimmy "Bug" Williams, Rudy Hackett, Chris Sease, and Jimmy Lee electrified the Manley faithful with a season-ending eleven wins in a row, propelling them into their third consecutive NCAA tournament. The Orange defeated La Salle in Philadelphia, 87-83 in overtime, and moved to the Providence Civic Center, where they beat the University of North Carolina 78-76 on a Lee basket with three seconds remaining. A 95-87 win over Kansas State in overtime sent the Cinderella Orangemen to their first Final Four, held in San Diego. Their bubble burst against the University of Kentucky, where the Orange lost, 95-79. But Danforth was named the Eastern Coach of the Year, and Hackett was named the ECAC's Player of the Year.

Roy Danforth.

Dennis DuVal,
ca. 1970.

Daily Orange, March 20, 1975.

Louis Orr (no. 55) and Roosevelt Bouie (no. 50). Photograph by Bruce Johnson.

In March 1976, Danforth resigned to become head coach at Tulane University. He was succeeded by his assistant, Jim Boeheim of Lyons, N.Y. The Boeheim era began with a bang, largely owing to the addition of two talented freshmen, Roosevelt Bouie and Louis Orr. In Boeheim's fourth game as head coach, the Orangemen upset number-one-rated Louisville in Louisville, 76-75. In each of his first four seasons as head coach, Boeheim took his team to the NCAA tournament, but despite the efforts of what became known as the "Bouie and Louie Show," in each of them they made an early exit. Many blamed these disappointments on the fact that during the regular season, the Orange did not play as many high-quality teams. That was about to change, however; at the end of the 1979 season, Syracuse announced that with six other teams it had joined a new league, the Big East.

Jim Boeheim.

"I'd recommend him for any job he wanted."

Roy Danforth on Jim Boeheim

The Orangemen responded to playing in the "Demi-Dome"—created when a fifty-yard section was cut from the Carrier Dome's football field with a sixty-foot-high curtain—both by continuing their winning tradition, and by setting several remarkable records for attendance. The Orangemen went to postseason play each year from 1981 to 1986—twice to the NIT in 1981 and 1982, and four times to the NCAAs. The story of the first half of the decade, however, was the electric play of Dwayne "Pearl" Washington. A freshman in the 1983–84 season, Washington sparked the team. Seven of their last conference games in his rookie season were decided at the buzzer or in overtime, including the Boston College contest where Washington's shot from

Dwayne "Pearl" Washington.

Daily Orange, March 30, 1987.

Celebration: 1987.

center court with no time left on the clock sealed the victory—it has gone down in Orange lore as simply "The Shot."

Washington garnered many honors for his play, but he left for the NBA at the end of his junior year. Everything pointed to a rebuilding year in 1986–87. Such was not to be. What turned into a magical season was accomplished by a fascinating mix of talent—sophomore Sherman Douglas, freshman Derrick Coleman, center Rony Seikaly, and seniors Greg Monroe and Howard Triche. They started the season at 15-0, and after a short slide, finished the season at 24-5. After losing to Georgetown in the finals of the Big East tournament, the Orangemen raced through the first rounds of the eastern regional bracket of the NCAA tournament. Both wins in the "Sweet 16"—over Florida and North Carolina—were heart-stoppingly close. The Final Four was held at the Superdome in New Orleans, and the Orange made quick work of their first opponent, the Providence Friars, 77-63. Boeheim would now coach for the national championship—the first national championship game for the Orange in basketball since 1925. The opponent was Indiana

University, and the game was a see-saw affair throughout. In the final four seconds, Indiana's Keith Smart made a jump shot to win the game, 74-73. In each of the final three seasons of the decade, the Orangemen went to the NCAA tournament, largely because of the play of Coleman, who in 1990 became the university's all-time leading scorer with 2,143 points, and its all-time rebounder—on the Hill *and* in the NCAAs.

"You won't see many better games."

Jim Boeheim to alumni, on the SU-Indiana championship game, 1987

The 1973 resignation of Ben Schwartzwalder began the Frank Maloney era at Syracuse. The former defensive line coach at the University of Michigan was, at thirty-three years old, one of the youngest head coaches in the nation. A strong

Frank Maloney.

believer in the power of positive thinking, Maloney tried to will his teams to win. He hoped to be helped by the addition of a new practice field, refurbished and renamed thanks to the $600,000 donation of Syracuse businessman J. Stanley Coyne. However, in his first five seasons, the Orangemen were a combined 22-32, despite the talents of quarterback Bill Hurley (who set eleven school records, including passing for 1,455 yards in 1977); Dave Jacobs (who would graduate tied for second place on the NCAA list for most career field goals); receiving sensation Art Monk; and running back Joe Morris, who in 1978 became the first freshman to rush for 1,000 yards. Maloney's job was clearly on the line. In 1979—a season spent entirely on the road because of the construction of the Dome—a 6-5 record earned the Orange a berth in the Independence Bowl, where they destroyed the McNeese State Cowboys, 31-7. Nevertheless, after christening the Dome with a 5-6 season in 1980, Maloney stepped down.

J. Stanley Coyne and Chancellor Eggers announce the gift for what would become Coyne Field, July 12, 1974.

Bill Hurley.

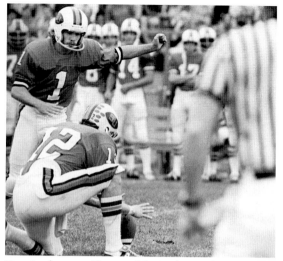

Dave Jacobs, 1975. Photograph by Paul Jasienski.

Joe Morris.

Maloney's successor was Dick MacPherson, a former defensive coach for the NFL Denver Broncos and Cleveland Browns. His first season was Joe Morris's last; the 4-6-1 record did not overshadow Morris's finishing as the university's all-time leading rusher with 4,229 yards. MacPherson's first three seasons were a combined 12-20-1. Then three things combined to turn the Orange

Coach Dick MacPherson, with Tony Romano.

football program around. The first was a huge win in the fourth game of the 1984 season, when the Orange stunned the number-one-ranked Nebraska Cornhuskers, 17-9. The Orange finished the 1984 season at 6-5, but the following season the second event occurred: sophomore Don McPherson had the opportunity to take over at quarterback. With him came the use of the option, a little-used offensive weapon for the Orangemen, who had been more used to the power-running style of Schwartzwalder and Maloney. Before his three years were up, McPherson owned every passing record at the university, and he was a runner-up in the 1986 Heisman Trophy balloting.

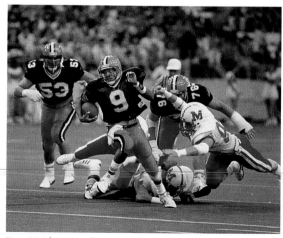

Don McPherson. Photograph by Stephen Parker.

The third event was the 1986 season. Undefeated and untied, the Orangemen, ranked fourth in the nation, played in the Sugar Bowl on New Year's Day, 1987. Their opponent was sixth-ranked Auburn. But the opportunity to present the university with its second undefeated season since 1959 fizzled with four seconds remaining on the clock, when Tigers coach Pat Dye elected to kick a field goal that tied the game. Angry Orange fans sent Dye some two thousand ties; Auburn fans sent sour grapes to Syracuse radio stations. MacPherson won the Bear Bryant Award as the college coach of the year. The rejuvenated Orange football program concluded the 1980s with three successive bowl appearances.

Here is a synopsis of the first undefeated season for the Orangemen since 1959, thanks to the March 1988 Syracuse University Magazine

Maryland (25-11): Tim Vesling kicked four field goals.

Rutgers (20-3): Ted Gregory's defense held Rutgers to 161 yards.

Miami (24-10): McPherson passed for 271 yards.

Virginia Tech (35-21): SU came back from a 21-7 halftime deficit. In the second half, the Hokies were held to –1 yards rushing.

Missouri (24-13): Capitalized on five Missouri fumbles; Rob Moore made a 71-yard touchdown run.

Penn State (48-21): With "the bomb"—an 80-yard game-opening touchdown—Rob Moore broke an eighteen-year losing streak against the Lions. MacPherson refused a ride on the shoulders of his players, so they carried out Schwartzwalder. (MacPherson: "I've never been carried off the field. I never want to be. It's a players' game." His reaction after the game: "God love everybody!")

Colgate (52-6): Tommy Kane—193 yards receiving and four touchdowns.

Pittsburgh (24-10): 441 yards of offense, including Rob Drummond's 91 yards of rushing.

Navy (34-10): 455 yards of offense.

Boston College (45-17): Came back from a 17-

point deficit with seven straight scores. After this game, they got their Sugar Bowl bid.

West Virginia (32-31): Perhaps the greatest game of Orange football since 1959. Ten seconds left on the clock—tight end Pat Kelly scored, and Michael Owens's two-point conversion kept the perfect season.

In 1971, Eggers established an intercollegiate athletic program for women. That same year, women's intercollegiate basketball began formal play. Under Coach Muriel Smith, who also served as the school's first field hockey coach, women's hoops went a combined 57-33, including a perfect 10-0 season in 1974–75. The sport experienced a breakout year in 1981, when the program moved to Division I status. Under third-year coach Barb Jacobs, and led by Libby McNulty and Jadeane Daye, the Orangewomen won a school record twenty-six games, only to be defeated in the national championship game of the Association for Intercollegiate Athletics for Women (AIAW) by the University of Kentucky, 86-63. The Orangewomen's first season in the Big East Conference of the NCAA came in 1983–84; the following year, led by freshman Felicia Legette, they won their first Big East title, defeating Villanova by one point. The Orangewomen went to the NCAA tournament that year and again in 1988. Before her 1988 graduation, Legette held university records for scoring (1,532) and rebounding (927). In fifteen seasons, Jacobs compiled a record of 229 victories.

Celebration after winning 1985 Big East Tournament.

1978 varsity crew, winning National Intercollegiate Rowing Championship. Photograph by Barry Wong.

In 1978, the varsity eight-oared shell won the National Intercollegiate Rowing Championship on Onondaga Lake. It was the Hill's first varsity rowing championship in fifty-eight years.

Yet in the end, it was not basketball or football or crew that was the university's most prolific sport in the Eggers era. Lacrosse transcended all the others. In 1971, Roy Simmons, Sr., retired as head coach and was replaced by his son. Roy Simmons, Jr.—nicknamed "Slugger" by his father because of his skill as a boxer—struggled through several

Randy Lundblad (no. 13) vs. Penn State, March 1984.

mediocre seasons in the first half of the decade. In 1979, spurred by the offensive power of attackman Tim O'Hara, the team dropped only four games and went to its first-ever NCAA tournament, where it lost in the first round. In 1983, however, the team lost only one game until being upended by Johns Hopkins in the semi-finals of the tournament. It was two more seasons before the Orange stunned the sports world by going 14-1, beating Hopkins 17-16 for the national championship—the first national championship in any sport for Syracuse University since the 1959 football season.

In 1987, the Orange acquired the services of Gary and Paul Gait, twin brothers from Brentwood Bay, British Columbia. They were arguably the greatest athletes ever to play a sport at Syracuse University; their names would become—and still are—equated with the sport of lacrosse around the nation. Many who saw Gary Gait soar from behind the goal, leaping over the crease for a score, are still in awe. In their four years at Syracuse, the Gaits led the Orangemen to three consecutive national championships. Between 1981 and 1990, the Orangemen assembled an astonishing 80-4 record.

With 1990 National Championship trophy. *Left to right:* Chancellor Eggers, Coach Roy Simmons, Jr., Athletic Director Jake Crouthamel. Photograph by Stephen Parker.

Cartoon from Joe Glisson, *Dome Sweet Dome.*

Outstanding Educators

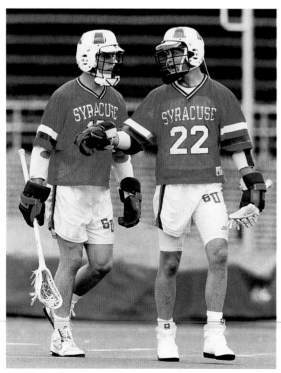

Gary (no. 22) and Paul Gait. Photograph by Stephen Parker.

Michael O. Sawyer, Political Science.

Tobias Wolff, Creative Writing Program, 1984.

Arthur Storch, Syracuse Stage, 1985.

Sol Gordon, Child and Family Studies, 1983.

Monsignor Charles Borgognoni. Photograph from the *Onondagan*, 1979.

Student Life

Computer Center, 1969.

Dorm life: Peck Co-op kitchen, 1971.

Ralph Ketcham, American Studies, CASE Professor of the Year, 1987.

Gebbie Speech and Hearing Clinic, 1973.

Dorm life: DellPlain Hall, 1976.

Streakers, from the *Onondagan*, 1974.

Dorm life: Sadler Hall, 1982.

Melvin Eggers, 1991.

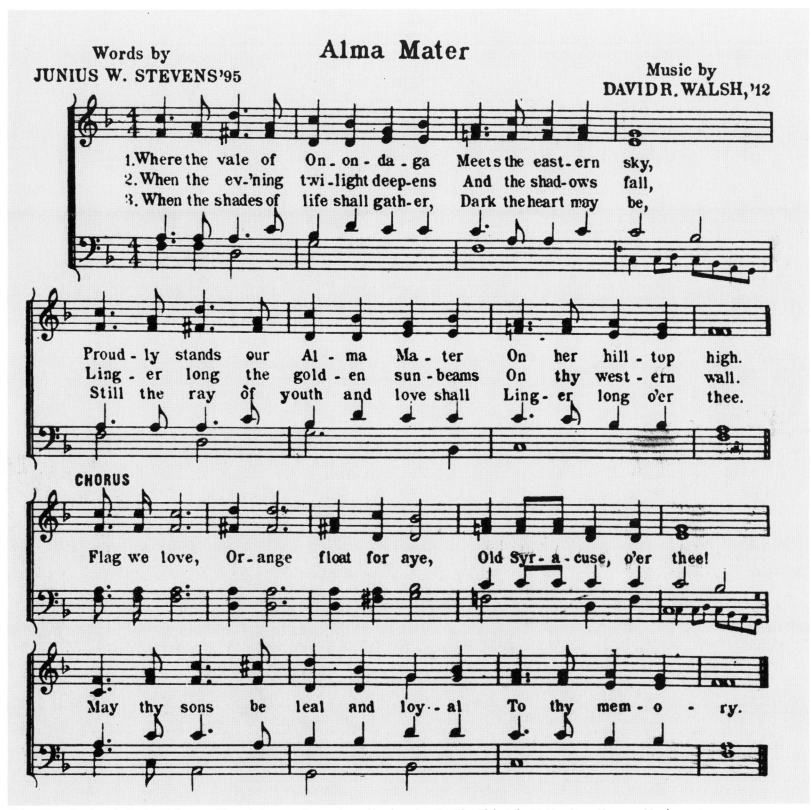

"Alma Mater," written by Junius W. Stevens, Class of 1895, was first performed by the university Glee Club at the Wieting Opera House on March 15, 1893.

Campus Life

Originally, the university's colors were rose pink and pea green. In 1873, the student body voted to change those colors to rose tint and azure—or the more colloquial pink and blue. After protest from athletes who felt less than combative wearing those colors to battle, the university decided to change its colors a third time. Around 1890, after a search revealed that no other college had chosen orange as its color, the Syracuse Orangemen were born.

The "Syracuse Orange."

One of the most hallowed traditions—cherished by math phobics to the present day—was the "Calculus Burial." To show their hatred of a course that was required of all graduates of the College of Liberal Arts, students buried their calculus books (later, they buried their general geometry texts and their analytical geometry texts, too). Up to 1876, the burials took place on Science Hill (near the present Crouse College); then they were done "at sea," in nearby Onondaga, Skaneateles, or Cazenovia Lakes— the textbook was placed on a raft, set on fire, and pushed out into the lake. The tradition extended into the 1960s.

Calculus Burial.

"Rushing" was a tradition that dated back to Genesee College. The purpose of the Salt Rush was "to take the freshness out of the first-year men." It began innocently enough, by sprinkling salt on the freshman seats in chapel. Then it got rough, as the frosh were pelted

with salt as they bolted down Crouse College hill. The Salt Rush spawned the Flour Rush, the Snow Rush, and the Orange Rush—all of which existed to pelt freshmen with foreign objects—and the Cane and Football Rushes, the object of which was for the frosh and sophs to maul

Salt Rush, 1903.

Flour Rush, undated.

Football Rush, 1912.

each other for possession of an object that was thrown in their midst.

In the 1890s, there was an annual football game between the freshman and the sophomore men; the losers forfeited their right to carry their canes on campus.

Yet there are some traditions that are more delicate—more romantic— in nature. Since 1912, tradition has held that a man and woman who kiss on what is colloquially known as the Kissing Bench, located on the west side of the Hall of Languages, will marry.

In 1932, sculptor Anna Hyatt Huntington presented her *Statue of Diana* to the university. For years, students rubbed the paw of Diana's dog for luck on their final examinations. The twelve-foot

Kissing Bench.

Ruth Blount, Women's Day May Queen, 1917.

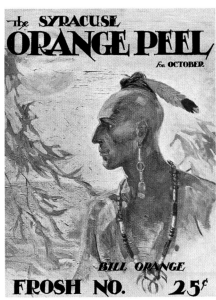

October 1931 *Orange Peel.*

Huntington *Statue of Diana.*

statue, originally placed in the main hall of Carnegie Library, is now located in Bird Library.

One of the great time-honored traditions of the first half of the twentieth century was Women's Day. Held in May, the day began with a break-

fast of strawberries, rolls, and coffee, served on the Old Stone Bridge of Yates Castle. It was followed by a field hockey game on Hendricks Field, a pageant featuring the May Queen (who had been elected from the senior class), and the presentation of the Junior Medal (sponsored by Eta Pi Upsilon and given to the most representative junior coed).

Throughout the first half of the century, freshmen were required to wear beanies on campus; when the command "Tip it, Frosh!" was given, woe to the freshman who refused. The tradition diminished in the mid-1950s, when more sophisticated World War II veterans refused to comply with upperclassmen's orders.

In 1931, a story that turned out to be a hoax became a part of the lore of the university. The October 1931 issue of the *Orange Peel* claimed that the bones of a sixteenth-century Indian—"the Saltine Warrior, Big Chief Bill Orange"—had been found buried under the foundation of the Women's Gymnasium. This story led to the adoption of the Indian as

Wilma Chidester, Women's Day May Queen, 1952.

Freshman beanies.

Saltine Warrior.

the mascot of the university. Although many suspected that the piece was a hoax, the issue was not put to rest until 1976, when Burges Johnson, the author of the story, admitted that it was a complete fabrication. Regardless, the Saltine Warrior would serve as the official mascot of the university for more than five decades.

The original Saltine Warrior would not be the only mascot in the life of the university . . .

Artist's rendering of the new Saltine Warrior (undated).

The Saltine Warrior as gladiator, 1978.

Otto the Orange.

Mascot, tradition, or sports story? All converged in the person of Dottie Grover. Twirling her baton to the rhythm of what was universally accepted as one of the nation's best marching bands, Grover achieved celebrity status in the 1950s that rivaled that of the football players. Dottie and her band—nicknamed "One Hundred Men and a Girl"—were often cheered louder than the football team.

Dottie Grover.

Some of the most hallowed traditions on the Hill revolved around the Greek houses. The tower of Crouse College housed a set of nine bells, all set to E-flat; the largest weighed three thousand pounds.

Every day, at least twice a day (with the exception of the World War II years), the men of Delta Kappa Epsilon (the Dekes) rang the Crouse College Chimes. At five o'clock every evening, the chimes played the alma mater; a concert followed every football game, followed by the tolling of the score.

Crouse Chimes.

Ringing of chimes, ca. 1943.

Step Singing was also a venerable tradition, in which choruses representing each sorority and women's dorm competed against one another in song on the steps of Hendricks Chapel.

Step Singing.

ATO cannon.

Starting in 1922, members of the Alpha Tau Omega house fired a cannon after every Orange touchdown and football victory. The ATO cannon was also used to kick off pep

Homecoming Queen competition in Maxwell Auditorium, ca. 1940.

rallies. The tradition died in 1960 during the Penn State game, when the cannon blast triggered a second explosion, sending one student flying some twenty feet with his clothes on fire.

Homecoming Weekend, and the choice of the Homecoming King and Queen, was an autumn tradition that dated back to the 1920s.

Homecoming Queen finalists, outside Maxwell Hall, ca. 1940.

Charla Hill, Homecoming Queen, 1988.

The Goon Squad was formed by the Traditions Commission in 1947 as its enforcement agency for a vast number of rituals. But as the 1960s killed off most of the old traditions, the Goons evolved into the institution's official "Welcome Wagon,"

helping new freshmen settle into their dorms and orienting them to campus. The Goons also put on a yearly show that satirized campus life.

Goon on opening day, 1969.

Muscular Dystrophy Dance Marathon, 1973.

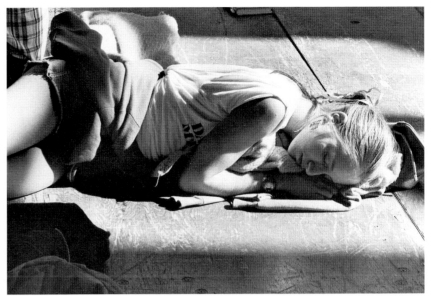

Muscular Dystrophy Dance Marathon, 1974.

William Johnston, coordinator of the Dance Marathon, with Jerry Lewis at the 1977 Muscular Dystrophy National Telethon.

The Muscular Dystrophy Dance Marathon debuted in 1973; by 1980 it had raised over $600,000 for the charity.

But the granddaddy of all traditions of Syracuse University was Colgate Weekend. It was the most important, revered, and often frenzied tradition in the history of the institution. Celebrated in conjunction

with the fall football contest between the Orange and the Red Raiders, the weekend featured the more sedate decorating contests and parades—as well as the scalping of captured underclassmen, the dumping of Orange paint into Hamilton's Taylor Lake and the retaliatory dumping of red paint onto cars outside Archbold, the stealing of the ATO cannon, and the decorations of

1920: SU, 14, Colgate, 0.

the Saltine Warrior statue. The presidents of both institutions tried in 1947 to negotiate rules for the madness; they had no chance of success. The tremor of Colgate Weekend subsided only in 1961, when the two schools stopped playing each other in football.

"Scalping" of "captured" students, 1944.

Poster for the Colgate Dance, 1941.

From the Colgate Weekend residence-decorating contest, 1949.

Finish of the 1947 Colgate game at Archbold Stadium. Thanks to Walter "Slivers" Slovenski's fake kick, which he followed with a sixty-seven yard touchdown run, the Orange won, 7-0.

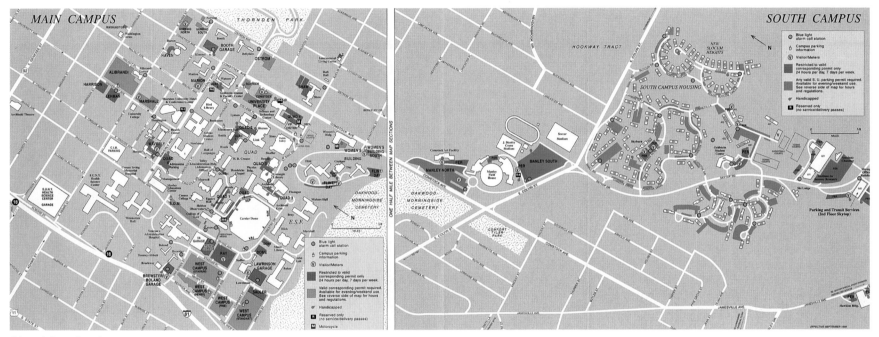

Map of the university, 1999.

Leadership

KENNETH A. SHAW, 1991–PRESENT

On April 20, 1991, Kenneth A. Shaw became the tenth chancellor of Syracuse University. Shaw did his undergraduate work at Illinois State University, where "Buzz" was his basketball nickname (in 1983, he was elected to the Illinois Basketball Hall of Fame). Studying sociology and psychology, he earned his master's at the University of Illinois and his doctorate at Purdue University. Shaw served as president of Southern Illinois University at Edwardsville, and served six years as chancellor of the Southern Illinois system before moving on to the University of Wisconsin system, where he was chancellor from 1986 to 1991. Like his predecessor, Shaw faced the fallout of the economic downturns of the early 1980s. His easygoing manner helped him when dealing with the demands of an institution that needed both restructuring and refocusing of its resources; as the Hill enters the next millennium, Shaw remains at the helm of a stronger, nationally competitive university.

Chancellor Kenneth Shaw.

Cartoon from Joe Glisson, *Dome Sweet Dome.*

"He looks like the all-American kid grown to maturity."

Syracuse Post-Standard, April 29, 1991

"I'm your very own chancellor, a job that requires wisdom, patience, empathy, a thick skin, and just enough class to be able to wear a hat like this and not feel like a complete fool."

Chancellor Shaw, during August 26, 1993, welcoming address to freshmen

Shaw at football game with students, September 21, 1991.

Chancellor Kenneth Shaw.

Transformation

Shaw stepped into a situation made critical by a severe financial crisis. Facing a projected 20 percent drop in enrollment and a budget shortfall of some $38 million, he moved quickly. In September 1991, after announcing that "we talk today of the beginnings of change," the chancellor told a packed meeting of the University Senate that early in the following year he would unveil the specifics of a plan to restructure the university significantly. That plan included cutting some 15 percent of the university's 4,300 employees and concurrently trimming the budgets of many schools, departments, and programs.

But Shaw also included in his announcement thirty-three initiatives designed to direct the institution toward becoming a more learning-based research institution. This began the institution's commitment to what would become known as the "Student-Centered Research University," termed "a state of mind" by the chancellor. Shaw also introduced programs to award efforts in undergraduate teaching, and a

Shaw, introduced to campus for the first time, April 25, 1991.

program was inaugurated to improve administrative services through employee training—Syracuse University Improving Quality (SUIQ).

"SU's Shaw Prepares for Revolution."

Headline in *Syracuse Herald-Journal*, May 4, 1991

Restructuring did not, however, slow the commitment of either the institution or its friends to the dream, begun under Eggers, of expanding the university's use of new technology. A $500,000 grant from Apple Corporation allowed for an increased use of computers in the classroom, and a new administrative mainframe was installed in Machinery Hall. Funding opportunities also led to more high-tech research opportunities. The university's Biomolecular Research Institute led the nation in inquiry in its field, as did the university's Gerontology Center, the recipient of a $2.3 million grant in September 1991. In September 1993, a three-year, $600,000 grant from the National Aeronautics and Space Administration established a Center for Hypersonics in the College of Engineering (hypersonics: the study of

Shaw at Senate meeting, November 11, 1991.

"The Student-Centered Research University."

SUIQ pin.

Computers in the classroom, ca. 1990.

flight at speeds near 4,000 mph). Two months later, a $1.8 million gift was made for the Earl V. and Josephine W. Snyder Innovation Management Center, formed to finance and support research efforts that bridged the themes of entrepreneurship and technology management with elements of leadership. In January 1994, thanks largely to the personal intervention of Shaw and New York Assemblyman Michael Bragman, the university's Research Park, a twenty-year project between the university and the Metropolitan Development Association (MDA), received $1.5 million in grants. Six months later, a $400,000 gift from Martin and Linda Yenawine of Fayetteville, New York, allowed for creation of the Yenawine Institute, formed to encourage partnerships between business leaders and social service providers to find practical solutions to social problems.

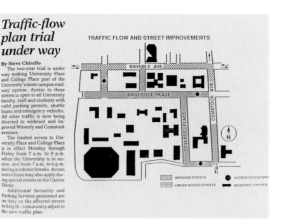

Map of the reconfiguration, from the *Syracuse Record*, August 22, 1991.

Left to right: Mildred Eggers, Chancellor Emeritus Eggers, Chancellor Shaw, Dean John L. Palmer of the Maxwell School, and Douglas Barclay, chairman of the Board of Trustees, at ground breaking for Eggers Hall, May 9, 1992.

Left to right: Dean William L. Pollard of the School of Social Work, Martin and Linda Yenawine, and Chancellor Shaw, on establishment of the Yenawine Institute, July 1994.

The physical plant of the institution also continued its path toward meeting modern needs. As a first step toward this development, in August 1991 the university reconfigured its road map. On a two-year trial basis, University Place and College Place were made part of the university's inner roadway system. All vehicle traffic was stopped on these streets, with the exception of cars with a valid parking permit, shuttles, and emergency vehicles. In November 1993, the Syracuse Common Council voted unanimously to make the new traffic pattern a permanent one.

The ground breaking for a major expansion of the Maxwell School took place on May 9, 1992. The

plan was to create what was billed as an "integrated social science complex" built around the old Maxwell Hall, a building that had been listed in the National Register of Historic Places, and which was to receive a complete renovation. By late December 1993, the move into the new building was largely completed; the building's dedication in January and October 1994 coincided with the university's celebration of its 125th anniversary, and Maxwell's 70th year jubilee. The new building, named for Melvin Eggers, showcased state-of-the-art technology for the social scientist.

Chancellor Shaw speaking at groundbreaking ceremony (*seated:* Chancellor Emeritus Eggers, Chairman Barclay).

Moving Holden Observatory to clear the site for Eggers Hall, June 26, 1991.

Eggers Hall, Maxwell School of Citizenship and Public Affairs.

Athletics

Along with the financial crisis, in 1991 Shaw inherited an athletic program stunned by charges of impropriety. By the end of that year, and throughout 1992, the university learned of the decisions of several NCAA investigations. Men's basketball was hardest hit: they could not play in the 1993 postseason, and had a reduction in both scholarships and off-campus visits. Also penalized were the wrestling and lacrosse teams.

In the midst of the NCAA probe, Manley Field House and Colvin Park got a facelift. Manley now featured a new football wing, an expanded training room, and a remodeled administrative wing; the park boasted two new football fields and a 400-meter, eight-lane running track. In June 1996, the 30,000-square-foot football wing was officially named for alumni William Petty and George R. Iocolano.

Chancellor Shaw cutting the 125th birthday cake, May 1995.

Left to right: Alumni Jerry Stiller, Dick Clark, and Henry Grethel at the 125th Anniversary Dinner, July 1995.

NCAA infraction news conference, October 1, 1992. *Left to right:* Athletic Director Jake Crouthamel, with coaches Jim Boeheim, Roy Simmons, Jr., and Ed Carlin.

In August 1994, the university began the celebration of its 125th anniversary. The following academic year was punctuated by a series of events designed to highlight the university's people, programs, and history. The celebration was capped off in July 1995 with a gala dinner at the Carrier Dome, featuring a full complement of past winners of the Arents Pioneer Medal, as well as many other friends and patrons of the university.

Left to right: Marty Glickman, John Mackey, and Jake Crouthamel, athletic director, at 125th Anniversary Dinner. Photograph from the *Syracuse Record*, July 24, 1995.

William Petty and George R. Iocolano Football Wing, Manley Field House.

The 1991 season was the first for Paul Pasqualoni; his team responded with a 10-2 season, capped off with a 24-17 victory over Ohio State in the January 1992 Hall of Fame Bowl. The 1992 season was the first year of the new Bowl Alliance in college football; the champion of the Big East Conference would now be guaranteed a berth in an Alliance bowl. The Orange won a bid to a tier-one bowl, the Fiesta, and it was one of the most exciting in recent memory. Trailing the Colorado Buffaloes 7-6 at the half, the Orange roared to a 20-point third quarter, capped by a 100-yard reverse kickoff return by Kirby Dar Dar. The Orange went on to win, 26-22; they finished their season at 10-2, ranked sixth in the nation. It was the Orangemen's sixth straight bowl victory.

Paul Pasqualoni. Photograph by Mike Okoniewski.

Left to right: Brian Piccuchi, David Walker, Terrance Wisdom, Marcus Lee, and Al Wooten with the Fiesta Bowl trophy, 1993. Photograph by Stephen Parker.

Hall of Fame Bowl. Photograph from the *Daily Orange,* January 1992.

The 1993 and 1994 seasons brought with them winning records, but no bowl invitations. Then Donovan McNabb began a four-year run at quarterback that would break every Orange record at the position. Between 1995 and 1998, the Orange were a combined 35-14, including two bowl victories (on January 1, 1996, at the Toyota Gator Bowl, the Orange overwhelmed ACC opponent Clemson, 41-0; in the 1996 Liberty Bowl, they swamped the University of Houston, 30-17) and two bowl defeats (in the 1998 Fiesta Bowl, they lost to Kansas State, 35-18; and in the 1999 Orange Bowl they lost to Florida, 31-10). McNabb's personal numbers were just as spectacular. McNabb tied the Syracuse University single-game record for touchdown passes (4), and set career records for touchdowns (96), total offensive yards (9,950), total offensive yards per game (221.1), and touchdown passes (77).

As they prepared for the 1999 season, the Syracuse Orangemen, entering their 109th season, had a 625-401-49 overall record, with nineteen bowl appearances (for a record of 10-8-1).

Donovan McNabb.

The Orange lacrosse team in the 1990s continued to perform as one of the premier programs in intercollegiate sports; the story of the stickmen in the 1990s was a story of an annual bid for the national title. Only one month after he took over as chancellor, Shaw saw the SU lacrosse team lose their bid for a fourth consecutive national championship. They were beaten at the Carrier Dome in the semifinals of the NCAA tournament by North Carolina, 19-13. The Orangemen reached the title game the following year, only to be defeated by Princeton, 10-9 in double overtime. But the national championship returned to the Hill in 1993, when the Orange won their fourth national title in six years, defeating North Carolina 13-12 on a breakaway goal by Matt Riter with only eight seconds left. In 1994, Virginia took the title from the Orange in the tournament quarterfinals, winning 15-14. But the following year, the Orange won back the championship with a 13-9 victory over Maryland at College Park. It was their fifth national championship in eight years, and their sixth overall. After an 11-10 loss to Princeton in the quarterfinals of the 1998

The 1995 national championship Orange lacrosse team.

mination of the underdog Orangemen, they were defeated by Kentucky, 76-67. At season's end, senior forward John Wallace was number three on the university's all-time scoring list and stood as the only player in SU history to score more than 800 points in one season.

"In the end, Kentucky earned the championship. But the Wildcats had to scratch and claw past a Syracuse team that believed in itself when few others did."

Syracuse Herald-Journal, April 2, 1996

John Wallace.

tournament, Roy Simmons, Jr., announced his retirement.

The 1991–92 season left Jim Boeheim with what the local newspaper called a "reconstruction project." That "project" made it to the NCAA tournament, only to lose to the University of Massachusetts, 77-71 in overtime. Ineligible for the following postseason because of NCAA sanctions, the 1992–93 Orange nevertheless posted a 20-9 record. Boeheim returned for the 1993–94 season with perhaps the best trio of starters in the nation: senior Adrian Autry, junior Lawrence Moten, and sophomore John Wallace. The 23-7 Orangemen went deep into the tournament, only to be disappointed in the West Regional semifinals, losing to Missouri, 98-88 in overtime. The 1994–95 Orange made their third consecutive overtime exit from the dance, losing to Arkansas 96-94.

Only two of 306 colleges and universities can hope to make it to the national championship game; in 1996, the Syracuse Orangemen did it for the second time in less than a decade. The Orange finished the 1995–96 season at 24-8, and entered the tournament on a wave of optimism. After disposing of Montana State and Drexel at Denver's McNichols Arena, the Orange defeated Georgia, 83-81, and then beat Kansas, 60-57, to advance to the Final Four. Storming into the Meadowlands to the strains of "The `Cuse Is in the House," the Orangemen disposed of Mississippi State 77-69. Despite the sheer deter-

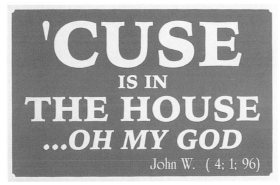

'CUSE IS IN THE HOUSE ...OH MY GOD

John W. (4; 1; 96)

"The 'Cuse Is in the House."

Jim Boeheim won his 500th game during he 1996–97 season, defeating Rutgers, 92-62. But the 19-12 Orangemen were snubbed by the NCAA tournament, and ultimately defeated in the first round of the NIT by Florida State, 82-67. Back in the NCAA tournament the following season, the Orange were ultimately defeated by Duke, 80-67.

"Boeheim has been at Syracuse for what seems to be eons. . . . He is an institution there, which suggests that pet rocks and lava lamps are probably big sellers in Syracuse still."

Michael Ventre, Los Angeles Daily News columnist

In 1993, Marianna Freeman, previously the head coach at Delaware State College, became the coach of the basketball Orangewomen. Two seasons later, she led the team to a share of the Big East 7 championship and a win over the defending national champion University of Connecticut at Manley Field House. In 1998–99, after being picked by the coaches to finish last in their division, the Orangewomen placed third in the Big East 7, with a league record of 7-11.

MOMENTS IN THE 1990S

1991: Philosophy professor Laurence Thomas spends $108.03 on a quarter-page advertisement in the *Daily Orange*, taking students to task for their academic passivity.

1992: The Muscular Dystrophy Association Dance Marathon celebrates its twentieth anniversary and collects more than $1 million in contributions.

1993: The Chancellor's Task Force on Student Rights and Responsibilities releases its report; as a result of its findings, Shaw approves major

Marianna Freeman.

changes in the way the university judicial system handles rape and sexual assault cases.

1994: Seana LaPlace becomes the first African-American woman elected president of the Student Government Association.

Seana LaPlace.

1995: Professor Stephen Macedo is the first person chosen to hold the Michael O. Sawyer Endowed Chair in Constitutional Law and Politics. Formerly at Harvard University and an expert in American constitutionalism and political theory, Macedo is chosen from more than one hundred candidates.

Left to right: Chancellor Shaw, Wendy Cohen, Ann Goldstein, and Alfred Goldstein at dedication of Goldstein Alumni and Faculty Center.

1996: Syracuse University wins the Theodore M. Hesburgh Award for Faculty Development to Enhance Undergraduate Learning.

1997: On October 31, the Goldstein Alumni and Faculty Center is dedicated. Formerly the Faculty Center, and before that the original house for the Delta Kappa Epsilon fraternity, the newly configured and renovated center features a new terrace on the main floor and the Chappell Conference Room.

1998: The Center for Really Neat Research (CRNR) is awarded a $1.6 million contract from the Defense Advanced Research Projects Agency to build a better land-mine detector. CRNR founder David J. Warner tells *Syracuse University Magazine* that the present detectors are "the same technology people use to comb the beaches of Florida."

1999: Students at the Newhouse School of Public Communications create a new television network. Called "Cow-TV" (for Collegiate Original Works Television), and created as a result of the output of a thesis course in the radio-television-film program, the network features only student work.

An Interview

In August 1999, Chancellor Shaw sat for an interview with me to complete this book. Originally, the subject of the interview was "The Future of Syracuse University"; however, as you will see, we took the opportunity to chat not only about that subject, but also about the focus of this book—the "views" of Syracuse University that he holds dear.

John Robert Greene and Chancellor Shaw during interview.

"It's Just a Fantastic Picture"

JOHN ROBERT GREENE: When you think of the visual character of this place, what comes to your mind?

CHANCELLOR SHAW: It's an architectural historian's delight. You can just about describe most of the eras of architecture in this country by looking at this university. It is architecturally eclectic—very interesting to tour. But the other way to see it is simply that it is a very beautiful place . . . where things *do* fit together, and care has been taken to ensure the integrity of the campus.

GREENE: What is your favorite view of the university?

SHAW: To be in the penthouse of the Management School, looking out toward the campus. And when you do that, you see our favorite buildings—Hall of Languages, Crouse, Tolley [Administration Building] . . . and you can look to your left and see Newhouse and Schine . . . and you can look beyond, and see the hills of Onondaga. It's just a fantastic picture. You get the whole feel of this being an aesthetically beautiful place.

View from penthouse of the Crouse-Hinds School of Management Building.

GREENE: Looking at them from the outside, what's your favorite building?

SHAW: It would be a tie between the Hall of Languages and Crouse [College], because they describe an important part of our past, but at the same time they're today and tomorrow. They're such magnificent structures, and a good reminder of our history.

GREENE: When you think of the university *today*, what do you think of?

SHAW: As I look out today, I see a marvelous physical plant that's been kept up, and we've tried very hard to make more beautiful, with all the walkways and the bricking. I see an institution that has clearly become a nationally competitive institution. I see, programmatically, the values we ascribe to being carried out.

GREENE: What are your thoughts on the immediate *future* of the institution?

SHAW: A board member asked me in May [1999] what our biggest challenge was. It was easy for me to respond. It is the aspirations we have for the university and where we are in those aspirations, and the tension that we create for ourselves in trying to continually move forward. It seems that as our achievements grow, our aspirations increase—and that's our biggest challenge.

GREENE: How do you plan to confront that challenge?

SHAW: In three ways. First is the allocation of our resources. We've come out of a period of restructuring, and fiscally we are very strong. Even though we now have a strong financial base and a balanced budget, we are going to have to make some very hard choices as to how we are going to spend that money . . . as opposed to making hard choices about reducing. And that's a different kind of challenge, but it's not necessarily any easier. The second area that is going to be extremely important in the next decade is what we do with respect to space planning. While we do have a very handsome physical plant, in terms of our aspirations, we're going to need to do quite a bit of remodeling . . .

GREENE: Do you have any plans in mind for this remodeling?

SHAW: A number of decisions center around what we do with Carnegie Library. What we do know is that we want to make it a learning center for the twenty-first century. Yes it will be a library, but it will be less a library in the conventional sense, because libraries have changed so greatly. Libraries have become true learning centers . . . now with over eight-hundred of our journals being accessed electronically. And there is another set of decisions that revolve around what to do with the Biology Department [currently located in Lyman Hall and the Biological Research Laboratory]. It'll take six to ten years to complete the effort. The end result will impact the entire campus, and the major decisions still need to be made.

GREENE: And the third way?

SHAW: The third way is fund-raising. We can't achieve our aspirations at our present level of funding. This is not to complain—there's nothing wrong with being a nationally competitive university—but we're not satisfied. We also know where our competitors are in terms of their endowments and their reserves—and this is why I talk about doubling the size of what we have. And that is going to require a very strong effort on our part. Those are the three things that are really going to drive the institution in the future.

GREENE: Clearly, the development of our technological and research base has been a key focus of your administration. Where do you see that effort heading in the next decade?

SHAW: It is a changing landscape that happens so quickly. Whatever you do, you are still behind the learning curve. Having said that, my view of the future in technology is that institutions like Syracuse will have some programs which you will be able to access through distance education. We are already at the point that you can have a lecture given live here, and people at Lubin House are receiving it . . . such that a very lively educational experience is going on. The biggest transformation is already appearing on campus—the use of technology to greatly improve the learning experience for resident students.

GREENE: How about Syracuse University as a research institution in the new millennium?

SHAW: During restructuring, while we decreased the number of faculty we have, it's interesting to

note that the number of sponsored programs stayed about the same—that's quite an accomplishment. But what we are going to have to do in terms of research is to push high scholarly productivity from all of our faculty—and the beauty

Prof. Bob Birge with Gel Cube.

Prof. Charles Driscoll and graduate student.

of this place is that we're willing to define scholarship in more realistic terms. A scholar in art and design isn't necessarily using the same tools as a scientist or a historian, and we're willing to

The "Scholarship of Teaching."

Marshall Street, August 1981.

acknowledge that, and not expect that there's a cookie-cutter approach to measuring scholarly productivity. What we also need to do is to focus our energies so that our areas are better defined and better supported. We need to be very focused on what we are doing, to focus our research strengths, as opposed to assuming that every one of our programs is going to attain national prominence.

GREENE: Then you are not necessarily talking about scholarly work in the more traditional sense . . .

Marshall Street, 1971.

SHAW: Yes, there is more. One form of scholarship is the scholarship of teaching. The definition of it is not "this is a good teacher" . . . but a person whose scholarship is understanding how people learn and using it to educate others. It is important to depict scholarship broadly.

GREENE: What about the relationship between the community and the university?

SHAW: We have about thirty-five sections of our writing program where the students are doing community service and then writing about it. Management requires much the same thing—in fact, there are *many* classes that require community service. We are talking about massive enrichment of the Central New York area by volunteers who come from this place. We did a survey for the 125th anniversary of the number of hours in one year that we had in volunteer work. We came up with 500,000 hours and stopped counting; and I think that's not an atypical year.

Part of our community involvement will be the renovation of Marshall Street, with the movie theater, the moving of power lines underground, and the establishment of BIDs (Business Improvement Districts).

GREENE: Let's close with this: do you have a favorite photo of this place?

SHAW: Yes. It's this one . . .

Suos Cultores Scientia Coronat
"Knowledge Crowns Those Who Seek Her"

Motto, Syracuse University

Crouse College.

Index

Page numbers in italics denote illustrations.